Siblings
Without
Rivalry

OTHER BOOKS BY ADELE FABER & ELAINE MAZLISH

Between Brothers and Sisters:
A Celebration of Life's Most Enduring Relationship

Liberated Parents/Liberated Children:
Your Guide to a Happier Family

How to Talk So Kids Will Listen &
Listen So Kids Will Talk

How To Talk So Kids Can Learn—
at Home and at School

How to Be the Parents You Always Wanted to Be

How to Talk So Teens Will Listen & Listen So Teens Will Talk

BOOKS FOR CHILDREN

Bobby and the Brockles

Bobby and the Brockles Go to School

Visit Adele Faber and Elaine Mazlish at
www.fabermazlish.com.

Siblings *Without* Rivalry

*How to Help Your Children
Live Together So You Can Live Too*

Adele Faber & Elaine Mazlish

W. W. Norton & Company
New York · London

Copyright © 2012, 1998, 1987 by Adele Faber and Elaine Mazlish

"Brothers and Sisters, After All" by Adele Faber and Elaine Mazlish, originally published in *Between Brothers and Sisters: A Celebration of Life's Most Enduring Relationship* (1989). Reprinted by permission of Adele Faber, Elaine Mazlish, and Philip Lief Group.

For information about permission to reproduce selections from this book, write to Permissions, W. W. Norton & Company, Inc., 500 Fifth Avenue, New York, NY 10110

For information about special discounts for bulk purchases, please contact W. W. Norton Special Sales at specialsales@wwnorton.com or 800-233-4830

Manufacturing by Courier Westford
Book design by Judith Abbate
Production manager: Louise Mattarelliano

Library of Congress Cataloging-in-Publication Data

Faber, Adele.
   Siblings without rivalry : how to help your children live together so you can live too / Adele Faber & Elaine Mazlish.
   p. cm.
   Rev. ed. of: Siblings without rivalry : how to help your children live together so you can live too. c1998.
   Includes bibliographical references and index.
   ISBN 978-0-393-06338-7 (hbk.) — ISBN 978-0-393-34221-5 (pbk.) 1. Child rearing.
2. Sibling rivalry. 3. Brothers and sisters. I. Mazlish, Elaine. II. Title.
   HQ769.F212 2012
   649'.143—dc23

                                                                      2011053243

W. W. Norton & Company, Inc.
500 Fifth Avenue, New York, N.Y. 10110
www.wwnorton.com

W. W. Norton & Company Ltd.
Castle House, 75/76 Wells Street, London W1T 3QT

1 2 3 4 5 6 7 8 9 0

*To all the grown-up siblings who still
have a hurt child inside them.*

Contents

Behold how good and how pleasant it is
for brothers and sisters to dwell together in unity.

THE BOOK OF PSALMS

We'd Like to Thank . . .

Our husbands, for their ongoing support and encouragement of this project. They were a daily source of strength to us, especially when the going was slow.

Each of our offspring, who as young children provided us with the raw material for this book and who, as young adults, gave us valuable suggestions about what we might have done differently.

The parents in our groups for their willingness to explore with us and try out this "new approach" with their children. Their experiences and insights enrich these pages.

Everyone who shared with us their past and present feelings about their brothers and sisters.

Kimberly Ann Coe, our artist, who somehow was able to sense exactly what we were after in our cartoon illustrations, and create a lovable cast of parents and children.

Linda Healey, for being a writer's dream editor, strong in her support of her authors' message and style, gentle and persistent in her pursuit of excellence.

Robert Markel, for his unwavering support throughout our career and for his taste and judgment on which we've come to rely.

And finally, our mentor, the late Dr. Haim Ginott, who gave us our first vision of how the flames of sibling rivalry could be reduced to a small, safe flicker.

How This Book Came to Be

As we were writing *How To Talk So Kids Will Listen & Listen So Kids Will Talk,* we ran into trouble. The chapter on sibling rivalry was getting out of hand. We were only halfway through, and it was already over a hundred pages long. Desperately we went to work to shorten, tighten, eliminate—anything to get it into proportion with the rest of the book. But the more we cut, the more unhappy we became.

Gradually the truth dawned on us. To do justice to sibling rivalry, we'd have to give it a book of its own. Once that decision was made, the rest fell into place. We would put into *How To Talk* . . . enough material on handling conflicts to ease parents over the roughest spots. But in our "sibling book" we would have room to stretch out, to tell about our early frustrations with our own battling kids; to describe the eye-opening principles we learned from the late child psychologist, Dr. Haim Ginott, in the years that we were part of his parent group; to share the insights we gained from our families, our reading, and our endless discussions with each other; and to describe the experiences of the parents who took part in the workshops we subsequently created and conducted on sibling rivalry.

It also occurred to us that we had an unusual opportunity through our nationwide speaking engagements to find out what parents around the country felt about sibling problems. We soon discovered we had a hot topic on our hands. Wherever we went, the very mention of the words "sibling rivalry" triggered an immediate and intense reaction.

"The fighting drives me up the wall."

"I don't know what'll happen first. Either they'll kill each other or I'll kill them."

"I get along fine with each child individually, but when the two of them are together, I can't stand either one of them."

Evidently the problem was widespread and deeply felt. The more we talked to parents about what went on between their children, the more we were reminded of the dynamics that produced such high levels of stress in their homes. Take two kids in competition for their parents' love and attention. Add to that the envy that one child feels for the accomplishments of the other; the resentment that each child feels for the privileges of the other; the personal frustrations that they don't dare let out on anyone else *but* a brother or sister, and it's not hard to understand why in families across the land, the sibling relationship contains enough emotional dynamite to set off rounds of daily explosions.

We wondered, "Was there anything to be said on behalf of sibling rivalry? It certainly wasn't good for parents. Was there something about it that might be good for children?"

Everything we read made a case for the uses of some conflict between brothers and sisters: From their struggles to establish dominance over each other, siblings become tougher and more resilient. From their endless rough-housing with each other, they develop speed and agility. From their verbal sparring they learn the difference between being clever and being hurtful. From the normal irritations of living together, they learn how to assert themselves, defend themselves, compromise. And sometimes, from their envy of each other's special abilities, they become inspired to work harder, persist and achieve.

That's the best of sibling rivalry. The worst of it, as parents were quick to tell us, could seriously demoralize one or both of the children and even cause permanent damage. Since our book was going to be concerned with preventing and repairing any kind of damage, we felt that it was important to look once again at the causes of the constant competition among siblings.

Where does it all begin? The experts in the field seem to agree that at the root of sibling jealousy is each child's deep desire for the *exclusive* love of his parents. Why this craving to be the one and only? Because from Mother and Father, that wondrous source, flow all things the child needs to survive and thrive: food, shelter, warmth, caresses, a sense of identity, a sense of worth, of specialness. It is the sunlight of parental love and encouragement that enables a child to grow in competence and slowly gain mastery over his environment.

Why wouldn't the presence of other siblings cast a shadow upon his life? They threaten everything that is essential to his well-being. The mere existence of an additional child or children in the family could signify LESS. Less time alone with parents. Less attention for hurts and disappointments. Less approval for accomplishments. And most frightening of all, the thought: "If Mom and Dad are showing all that love and concern and enthusiasm for my brother and sister, maybe they're worth more than me. And if they are worth more, that must mean that I'm worth less. And if I am worth less, then I'm in serious trouble."

No wonder children struggle so fiercely to be *first* or *best*. No wonder they mobilize all their energy to have *more* or *most*.

Or better still, ALL. Security lies in having all of Mommy, all of Daddy, all the toys, all the food, all the space.

What an incredibly difficult task parents confront! They have to find the ways to reassure each child that he or she is safe, special, beloved; they need to help the young antagonists discover the rewards of sharing and cooperation; and somehow they have to lay the groundwork so that the embattled siblings might one day see each other as a source of pleasure and support.

How were parents coping with this heavy responsibility? In order to find out, we devised a brief questionnaire.

Is there anything you do with your children that seems to help their relationship?

Is there anything you do that seems to make it worse?

Do you remember what your parents did that increased the hostility between you and your siblings?

Did they ever do anything that decreased the hostility?

We also asked about how they got along with their siblings when they were young, how they get along now, and what areas they'd like to see covered in a book on sibling rivalry.

At the same time we interviewed people personally. We recorded hundreds of hours of conversations with men, women, and children of diverse backgrounds ranging in age from three to eighty-eight.

Finally we gathered together all our materials, old and new, and ran several groups of eight sessions each on sibling rivalry alone. Some of the parents in these groups were enthusiastic right from the start; some were skeptical ("Yeah, but you don't know *my* kids!"); and some were at their wits' end, ready to try anything. All of them participated actively—taking notes, asking questions, role-playing in class and bringing back to each other the results of their experiments in their home "laboratories."

From all these sessions and from all the work we had done in the years before comes this book, the affirmation of our belief that we, as parents, *can* make a difference.

We can either intensify the competition or reduce it. We can drive hostile feelings underground or allow them to be vented safely. We can accelerate the fighting or make cooperation possible.

Our attitude and words have power. When the Battle of the Siblings begins, we need no longer feel frustrated, crazed, or helpless. Armed with new skills and new understanding, we can lead the rivals toward peace.

Authors' Note

In order to simplify the telling of our story, we combined the two of us into a single person, our six children into two boys, and the many groups which we ran together and separately, into one. So much for rearranging reality. Everything else in this book—the thoughts, the feelings, the experiences—is exactly as it happened.

Adele Faber
Elaine Mazlish

Siblings *Without* Rivalry

── ONE ──

Brothers and Sisters—
Past and Present

I secretly believed that sibling rivalry was something that happened to other people's children.

Somewhere in my brain lay the smug thought that I could outsmart the green-eyed monster by never doing any of the obvious things that all the other parents did to make their kids jealous of each other. I'd never compare, never take sides, never play favorites. If both boys knew they were loved equally, there might be a little squabble now and then, but what would they really have to fight about?

Whatever it was they found it.

From the time they opened their eyes in the morning till the time they closed them at night, they seemed committed to a single purpose—making each other miserable.

It baffled me. I had no way to account for the intensity, savagery, and never-endingness of the fighting between them.

Was there something wrong with them?

Was there something wrong with me?

Not until I shared my fears with other members of Dr. Ginott's parent-guidance group did I begin to relax. It was pure happiness to discover that my misery had lots of company. Mine was not the only day punctuated by namecalling, tattling, punches, pinches, shrieks and bitter tears. I wasn't the only one walking around with a heavy heart, jangled nerves, and feelings of inadequacy.

You would think, having been young siblings ourselves once, that we would all have known what to expect. Yet most of the parents in the group were as unprepared as I for the antagonism between their children. Even now, years later, as I sit here leading my first workshop on sibling rivalry, I realize how little has changed. People can't wait to express their dismay at the disparity between their rosy expectations and rude reality.

"I had another child because I wanted Christie to have a sister, someone to play with, a friend for life. Well now she has her sister and she hates her. All she wants to do is 'send her back.'"

"I always thought my boys would be loyal to each other. Even though they fought at home, I was sure they'd stick together on the outside. I nearly died when I found out that my older son was part of a group at the bus stop that was ganging up on his little brother."

"As a man who grew up with brothers, I knew boys fought, but somehow I pictured girls getting along. Not my three. And the worst part is, they have memories like elephants. They never forget what 'she did to me' last week, last month, last year. And they never forgive."

"I'm an only child so I thought I was doing Dara a big favor when I had Gregory. I was naive enough to believe that they'd automatically get along. And they did—until he started to walk and talk. I kept telling myself, 'It'll get better as they get older.' If anything, it's gotten worse. Gregory is six now and Dara is nine. Everything that Gregory has, Dara wants. Everything Dara has, Gregory wants. They can't get within two feet of each other without kicking or hitting. And they both keep asking me, 'Why did you have to have him?' 'Why did you have to have her?' 'Why couldn't I be an only child?' "

"I was going to avoid sibling rivalry altogether by spacing the children properly. My sister-in-law told me to have them close together, that they'd be like puppies playing with each other. So I did and they fought all the time. Then I read a book that said the perfect spacing was three years apart. I tried that too, and the big one lined up with the middle one against the little one. I waited four years for the next one, and now they *all* come crying to me. The younger ones complain that the oldest is 'mean and bossy,' and the oldest one complains that the little ones never listen to him. There's no winning."

"I never understood why people worried so much about sibling rivalry, because I had no problem when my son and daughter were young. Well, they're teenagers now and making up for lost time. They can't be together for a minute without sparks flying."

As I listened to their collective distress, I found myself wondering, "What are they so surprised about? Had they forgotten their own childhood? Why couldn't they draw upon the memories they had of their relationships with their brothers or sisters? And how about me? Why weren't my experiences with my siblings more helpful to me when I was raising my own children? Maybe it was because I was the baby in the family, with a much older sister and brother. I had never seen two boys grow up together."

When I shared my thoughts with the group, people were quick

to agree that their children, too, were very different in number, spacing, sex and personality from the siblings with whom they had grown up. They also pointed out that our perspective was different. As one father wryly observed, "It's one thing to be the child doing the fighting. It's another being the parent who has to cope with the fighting."

Yet even as we were coolly commenting upon the distinctions between our past and present families, old and powerful memories began to surface. Everyone had a story to tell, and little by little, the room became filled with the brothers and sisters of yesterday and the strong emotions that marked those relationships:

"I remember how angry I used to get when my oldest brother made fun of me. My parents would tell me over and over again, 'If you don't respond, then he won't bother you,' but I always did respond. He'd tease me incessantly to make me cry. He'd say, 'Take your toothbrush and leave. Nobody loves you anyhow.' That always worked. I always cried on that one."

"My brother used to tease me, too. Once when I was about eight, I got so mad at him for trying to trip me while I was riding my bike that I said to myself, 'This is enough. This has got to stop.' Then I went into the house and called the operator. (I'm from a small town upstate, and we didn't even have dial phones back then.) I said, 'I'd like the police, please.' The operator said, 'Well, ummm . . .' and then my mother came in and told me to put the phone down. She never yelled at me, but she said, 'I'm going to have to speak to your father about this.'

"That night when he came home from work I pretended to be asleep, but he woke me up. All he said was, 'You can't handle your anger like that.' My first reaction was relief that I wasn't going to be punished. But afterwards, I remember lying there, feeling angry all over again. And helpless."

"My brother wasn't allowed to be mean to me, no matter what I did to him. I was 'Daddy's little girl.' I could get away with anything. And I did some pretty horrible things. Once I threw hot bacon grease on him. Another time I punctured his arm with a fork. Sometimes he'd try to stop me by holding me down, but when he let go, that's when I'd really hurt him. One day when my parents weren't home, he punched me in the face. I still have the scar under my eye. That was it. I never laid a hand on him after that."

"In my family fighting just wasn't permitted. Period. My brother and I weren't even allowed to get mad at each other. A lot of the time we really didn't like each other, but no, you couldn't get mad. Why? No reason. Just not allowed. It was, 'He's your brother. You *have* to love him.' I would say, 'But Ma, he's a pain in the neck and he's selfish!'

" 'Well too bad. You have to like him.'

"So a lot of my angry feelings got squished down, because I was afraid of what would happen if they ever came out."

As more people shared their sibling memories, I marveled at how each recounting seemed to catapult the teller back in time and summon up the old hurt and anger all over again. Yet how different were these scenarios from the ones the parents had described earlier between their own children? The setting and the characters weren't alike, but the feelings seemed very much the same.

"Maybe the generations aren't that different," someone commented ruefully. "Maybe we just have to learn to accept the fact that siblings are natural adversaries."

"Not necessarily," one father objected. "My brother and I had a very close relationship right from the beginning. When I was little my mother used to put him in charge of me, and he was always good-natured about it—even when she insisted that he see to it that I finish my bottle before he could go off to play. I didn't want to have to finish my bottle, and he didn't feel like waiting around, so he'd drink my bottle for me. Then we'd go out together and visit his friends."

Everyone laughed. A woman said, "That reminds me of my sister and me. We were always in cahoots, especially when we were teenagers. We used to band together whenever we wanted to punish my mother. If she scolded or reprimanded us, we'd go on a hunger strike—one at a time. This drove my mother crazy, because she used to worry about how thin we were. She was always making us drink egg nogs and milk shakes, so when we stopped eating that was the worst punishment for her. But unbeknownst to her, we really were eating. The one who wasn't on the hunger strike would bring food to the one who was."

She paused and frowned. "But my younger sister is another story altogether. I never liked her. She was born ten years after me, and the sun rose and set with 'the baby.' To me she was just a spoiled brat. And still is."

"That's probably what my older sisters would say about me," another woman said. "They were eight and twelve when I was born, and I think they were jealous because I was my father's favorite. Also I had a lot of advantages that they didn't. There was more money when I was born, and I was the only one who got to go to college. My sisters were both married at 19.

"Now since my father's death, my mother and I have become very close. She's also become close to my children. Recently we were talking about turning her house into a mother-daughter house, and you wouldn't believe what's going on. When my mother told my sisters about our plans, they hit the roof. '*We* had to get a mortgage when we bought a house . . . *We* had to struggle to get what we got all these years . . . *She* went to college . . . *Her husband* went to college . . . *He* has a good job.'

"I think what bothers me most, is that now my nieces and nephews are resentful of my children. They say, 'Grandma, how come you spend all your time with them? You never come to see us anymore!' The jealousy never seems to end. It's gone down from one generation to the next."

Sighs were heard throughout the room. Someone commented that we were dealing with "heavy stuff" here. I felt the need to sum up before we moved on: "We've been looking at our own childhood and our children's childhood, and what we seem to be saying so far is that our relationships with our siblings can have a powerful impact upon our early lives, producing intense feelings, positive or negative; that these same feelings can persist into our adult relationships with our brothers and sisters; and finally, that these feelings can even be passed on to the next generation."

There was more, but I didn't quite know what it was. Again I thought of my own brother and sister, and how they treated me like a "pesty" kid who was always in their way, and how even now, as a reasonably successful adult, I still sometimes see myself as being "in the way." Aloud I asked, "I'm wondering, would it be going too far to say that these early experiences with siblings could determine how we act or think or feel about ourselves today?"

There was barely a moment's hesitation. Four hands shot up at once. I nodded to one of the fathers.

"Absolutely!" he said. "I'm a person who has to be in charge.

And I'm sure it's because I was the oldest of my three brothers. I was the benevolent dictator over the younger boys. They always looked up to me and would do anything I told them. Sometimes I beat them up, but I also protected them from the bullies in the neighborhood.

"Even today, I have to be 'on top.' Recently I had an excellent offer to sell my business. The deal was for me to manage it for the new owners. But I know myself. I'll never do it. I've got to be the boss."

"I'm the youngest of five boys, and there's not a doubt in my mind that my brothers affect the way I think about myself today. They're all high-powered people, super-achievers—academically, athletically, you name it. Only to them it came naturally. When I was a kid, I was constantly trying to keep up with them. While they were having fun, I was upstairs grinding away at the books. They could never figure me out. They used to call me 'the adopted one'—affectionately of course.

"To this day I push myself. My wife accuses me of being a 'workaholic.' What she doesn't understand is that part of me is still running like hell to keep up with my brothers."

"I stopped trying to keep up with my older sister a long time ago," a woman said. "She was so beautiful and talented, there was never any contest. And she knew it.

"I remember once when I was around thirteen, we were dressing up to go to a family wedding. I thought I looked really nice. She stood next to me in the mirror and said, 'I'm the GGG girl—Gorgeous, Glamorous, and Glorious.' Then she looked at me and said, 'You're the SSS girl—'Sweet, Simple, and Sincere.' I've never forgotten it. To this day if anyone praises me, I think, 'Yeah, yeah, but you should meet my sister.'"

"I was affected by my sister, too," a woman said softly. Several people leaned forward to hear her. "She's always been . . . an embarrassment to me." She hesitated, took a breath, and went on. "From as far back as I can remember she's had emotional problems and was always doing weird things that I had to explain away to my friends. My parents were always so concerned about her that I felt I had to be the good one, the one they could depend upon. Even though I was the younger, I always felt like the older.

"The only change over the years is that my sister has gotten worse. And everytime I see her—even though I know it's not her fault—I feel resentful, as if she cheated me out of a normal childhood."

I listened in amazement. I had always been aware of the part that parents played in shaping their children's lives, but never until this moment had I considered how powerfully siblings could affect each other's destiny.

Yet here was one grown man saying he still has to be the boss; another who is still driving himself to keep up, a woman who still feels she can never measure up; and another who is still suffering from having to be "the good girl." And mainly because of who their siblings happened to be.

As I was busy trying to digest my new thoughts, I suddenly became aware that a man in the group had been speaking for a while. I forced myself to concentrate on what he was saying.

". . . so in my home it was my father who was the unstable one. My mother was very affectionate, very calm. But my father was a man of temper, a man of uncontrollable actions. He'd leave, saying he was going away for two days, and then he'd stay away for two months. So we all more or less huddled together to protect each other. The big ones looked after the little ones and we all took jobs after school as soon as we were old enough to work. Everybody pitched in with their earnings. If we all hadn't stuck together nobody would have made it."

A murmur ran through the room. "Mmmm . . . wonderful . . . beautiful." This last story had touched the group's deepest longings—to have children who would "be there" for each other with love, support, and loyalty.

One woman said, "That was inspiring! What you just described is everything I could ever hope for. But it's also discouraging. I've heard of other families where the kids pull together because the parents have serious problems. I'd hate to think that my husband would have to walk out on me in order for my kids to start being decent to each other."

"As I see it," a man commented, "the whole thing is a genetic crapshoot. If you're lucky, you get a winning combination of kids whose personalities go well together. If not, you're in trouble. But either way, folks, it's out of our hands."

"I don't accept that it's 'out of our hands,'" another woman retorted. "We heard a lot of examples here today of parents who made things worse between their kids, who actually drove them apart. I joined this group because I'd like my children to be friends someday."

Where had I heard those words before? Aloud I said, "You remind me of me ten years ago. Only I was crazed on the subject. I was going to see to it personally that my two boys became friends. As a result I found myself on an emotional roller coaster. Everytime they played together nicely, I was elated. I'd think 'There! They *do* like each other. I'm a wonderful mother.' And everytime they fought, I would despair. 'They hate each other, and it's my fault!' One of the happiest days of my life was the day I gave up the 'good friends' dream and replaced it with a more realistic goal."

The woman seemed confused. "I'm not sure I know what you're getting at," she said.

"Instead of worrying about the boys becoming friends," I explained, "I began to think about how to equip them with the attitudes and skills they'd need for all their caring relationships. There was so much for them to know. I didn't want them hung up all their lives on who was right and who was wrong. I wanted them to be able to move past that kind of thinking and learn how to really listen to each other, how to respect the differences between them, how to find the ways to resolve those differences. Even if their personalities were such that they never could be friends, at least they would have the power to make a friend and be a friend."

The woman seemed taken aback. I could see why. It had taken me a long time to make peace with what I had just summed up for her so swiftly.

"Please understand," I said, "there were plenty of times when I was too tired, too disgusted, or too angry at the kids to even make an effort. But when I was able to help them go from a shouting match to a rational discussion, I felt terrific—like a very competent parent."

"I don't know if I could do that," she said nervously.

"There's no mystery about what I did. Whatever skills I used, you can too," I reassured her. "And you will, beginning next week."

She broke into a weak smile. "I might not last till then," she said. "What do I do in the meantime?"

I spoke to the whole group now. "Let's use this week to observe what stirs things up between our kids. Don't let the discord go to waste. Write down the incidents or conversations that distress you. At our next meeting we'll share our findings and take it from there."

• • •

DRIVING HOME FROM the session I found myself thinking about my own sons, now grown. Still vivid in my mind is the conversation between them after last week's Thanksgiving dinner.

Suddenly I'm standing in my dining room again, clearing the table, listening to the two of them as they start the cleanup in the kitchen.

At first they joke about dividing up the chores, each claiming a different speciality and trading off the "yecch" jobs. Then the talk grows serious as they compare their colleges and their majors—one in science, the other, art. All at once a heated debate erupts about who is more important to society, the artist or the scientist. "Look at Pasteur." "Yeah, but look at Picasso." They go on and on, each trying to convince the other. Finally, worn down, they concede that *both* have value.

After a moment's lull the conversation turns back into the past. An old anger is raked up and they argue again about who did what to whom and why, each explaining himself anew from his grown-up position. After a while the mood changes again. Warm funny memories are trotted out, and both boys collapse into laughter.

It's almost as if two forces are at work: one pushing them apart as they use the differences between them to define their unique, separate selves; the other pulling them together so they can come to know their unique brotherhood.

As I half-listen from the next room, I am surprised at how

relaxed I am. I realize how little emotional investment I have in the moment-by-moment "temperature" of their relationship. I know that the differences in interests and temperament that kept them from being close in childhood are still there. But I also know that over the years I had helped them build the bridges to span the separate islands of their identities. If they ever need to reach each other, they have many ways of getting there.

TWO

Not Till the Bad Feelings
Come Out . . .

The next session started unofficially as people were taking off their coats. "You know it helped to take notes while the kids were fighting," a mother remarked. "I was so busy writing, I didn't even get upset."

"I wish I could say the same," another woman commented. "By the time the week was up, I could hardly look at my oldest daughter."

The woman picked up her notebook and opened it to the first page. "Would you like to hear a list of what she dished out to her little sister at breakfast this morning?

I'm glad I'm not sitting near you.

You smell.

Daddy likes me better than he likes you.

You're ugly.

You don't know the alphabet.

You need Mommy to tie your shoelaces.

I'm prettier than you."

There were groans of recognition from the others who were settling into their seats.

"I thought my son would outgrow that kind of childish cruelty," a father said wearily. "But he's a teenager now and still torments his brother. I wouldn't even repeat some of the things he calls him."

"I don't understand what makes some of them so mean," another woman said. "My five-year-old will pull the baby's hair, put his fingers up her nose, in her ears, in her eyes. The little one is lucky she's still got eyeballs."

I knew exactly what they all were talking about. I remember my own bewilderment and rage at finding the baby with two long scratches on his back and my three-year-old standing there with an evil little grin on his face. What a mean, rotten kid! Why would he do it?

To help us get in touch with the source of our children's "meanness," I handed out the following exercise for the group to work on (Dear Reader, you might find it useful to jot down your own reactions. If you're a man, substitute "husband" for "wife" and "he" for "she" throughout the exercise):

• • •

IMAGINE THAT YOUR SPOUSE puts an arm around you and says, "Honey, I love you so much, and you're so wonderful that I've decided to have another wife just like you."

Your reaction: _____

When the new wife finally arrives, you see that she's very young and kind of cute. When the three of you are out together, people say hello to you politely, but exclaim ecstatically over the newcomer. "Isn't she adorable! Hello sweetheart . . . You are precious!" Then they turn to you and ask, "How do you like the new wife?"

Your reaction: _____

The new wife needs clothing. Your husband goes into your closet, takes some of your sweaters and pants and gives them to her. When you protest, he points out that since you've put on a little weight, your clothes are too tight on you and they'll fit her perfectly.

Your reaction: _____

The new wife is maturing rapidly. Every day she seems smarter and more competent. One afternoon as you're struggling to figure out the directions on the new computer your husband bought you, she bursts into the room and says, "Oooh, can I use it? I know how."

Your reaction: _____

When you tell her she can't use it, she runs crying to your husband. Moments later she returns with him. Her face is tear-stained and he has his arm around her. He says to you, "What would be the harm in letting her have a turn? Why can't you share?"

Your reaction: _____

One day you find your husband and the new wife lying on the bed together. He's tickling her and she's giggling. Suddenly the phone rings and he answers it. Afterwards he tells you that something important has come up and he must leave immediately.

He asks you to stay home with the new wife, and make sure she's all right.

Your reaction: _____

Did you find that your reactions were less than loving? The people in our group readily admitted that beneath their respectable, civilized exteriors lurked a capacity for pettiness, cruelty, spite, and thoughts of vengeance, torture, and murder. Even those who thought of themselves as being secure and having high self-esteem were surprised to find how enraged and threatened they could feel by the very presence of the "other."

"Something bothers me," a woman said. "This exercise implies that it's only the first born who reacts this way. In my house it's the baby who feels threatened and angry. She's only eighteen months old, but she'll attack her four-year-old brother with no provocation. Yesterday she came up from behind while he was watching television and bopped him on the head with her maracas. And just this morning she was lying on the bed with me, peacefully drinking her bottle, but the second her brother tried to lie down on the other side of me, she stopped drinking and gave him such a shove he landed on the floor."

A long discussion then ensued about the feelings of the younger child. Several other parents spoke of having feisty younger children who felt the need to challenge the older ones from early on. Still others described young children who worshipped an older brother or sister, and were hurt and confused by their sibling's rejection. And one parent told of a youngest child who was overwhelmed and discouraged because he felt he would never catch up.

One father seemed annoyed by the direction of our discussion. "Frankly," he said, "I think there's been too much pandering to feelings. I know I've had it up to here with all the emotionalism in the house. I come home at the end of a long day—the three girls are screaming at each other, my wife is screaming at them, and they all come running to me to complain about each other. I don't want to hear from anybody about who feels what or why! I just want it ended."

"I hear your impatience and frustration," I said. "Yet here's the irony. If we're to have any hope of 'ending it,' then the very emotions that we want to close the door on and lock out, need to be invited in, made welcome, and treated with respect."

He sat there scowling at me.

"I know how upsetting it can be," I said, "to hear one child rage against another. But if we forbid the expression of that rage, the danger is that it will go underground and reappear in other forms, either as physical symptoms or emotional problems."

Now he looked skeptical.

"Let's see what happens to us as grown-ups," I said, "when negative feelings aren't permitted. Let's go back for a moment to the new husband/new wife analogy. Suppose . . ."

"I had trouble with that one," another man interrupted. "After all, it isn't the cultural norm in America for people to take on a second spouse. It isn't even legal. Whereas it is normal and legal for parents to have more than one child."

"Granted," I said, "but for the sake of this exercise, let's say that the cultural norms were changing, and that this second marriage of yours has been decreed by law. Because of a shortage of males or females in the land, new legislation has been passed making it mandatory for the scarcer sex to take on another spouse."

"Okay," he said grudgingly. "I could go along with that."

"Why wouldn't you?" a woman quipped. "You're the scarcer sex!"

I waited for the laughter to subside. "It's been a year now," I continued, "since the new wife or new husband came into the house. Instead of getting used to his or her presence, you feel even worse about it. Sometimes you wonder if there's something wrong with you. As you're sitting at the edge of your bed, filled with hurt and pain, your mate walks into the room. Before you can stop yourself you blurt out, *"I don't want that person in this house anymore. It's making me very unhappy. Why can't you get rid of her/him?"*

Your husband or wife will respond in a variety of ways. Note your reaction to each of the following statements:

1. That's nonsense. You're being ridiculous. You have no reason to feel that way.

Your reaction: _____

2. You make me very angry when you talk like that. If that's the way you feel, please keep it to yourself, because I don't want to hear it.

Your reaction: _____

3. Look, don't put me in a position where I have to do the impossible. You know very well I can't get rid of him (her). We're a family now.

Your reaction: _____

4. Why must you be so negative all the time? Find a way to get along and don't come running to me with every little thing.

Your reaction: _____

5. I didn't only marry again for myself. I know you're lonely sometimes and I thought you'd like some companionship.

Your reaction: _____

6. Come on, honey. Cut it out. What do my feelings for you have to do with anyone else? There's enough love in my heart for both of you.

Your reaction: _____

Once again the group was taken aback by their reactions. Some said they felt, "stupid," "guilty," "wrong," "crazy," "defeated," "powerless," "abandoned."

Others said, "The real me is unacceptable" . . . "I must be a bad person" . . . "I have to pretend to be happy with this situation in order to keep the little bit of love that's left to me" . . . "There's no one to talk to, no one who cares."

But the feeling that surprised everyone the most was the burning desire to do harm, no matter what the cost. They wanted to get the newcomer into trouble, to hurt her or him physically. It didn't matter if they hurt themselves in the process or invoked the wrath of their spouse. It would be worth it if they could diminish the intruder in the eyes of their mates. What's more, they wanted to hurt their mates too, to punish them for inflicting this misery upon them.

And yet as we looked at what was said to cause this "outsized" reaction, we had to admit that it was nothing very unusual. It is common practice to deal with another person's "unreasonable" emotions with denial, logic, advice or reassurance.

When I asked the group what they would want their mates to do, they answered in savage unison. "Get rid of her!" "Get rid of him!" There were gleeful guffaws followed by some serious second thoughts.

"If my husband 'got rid of her' just because I asked him to, I'd be scared. I'd figure he could do the same to me one day."

"My husband would have to tell me that he loves me best and that she means nothing to him."

"I might buy that for the moment, but afterwards I'd begin to wonder whether he gives her the same line about me."

"Then what would it take to satisfy you people?" I asked jokingly.

There was a brief pause. Then:

"I'd want the freedom to say all kinds of nasty, critical things about the new wife—whether they were true or not—and not once have him defend her, or put me down, or get angry."

"Or look at his watch."

"Or turn on the TV."

"The main thing for me would be to know that he really understood how I felt."

It suddenly occurred to me that most of the responses were coming from the women in the group. Was it because I had slanted the exercise more toward the "new wife" than the "new husband?"

Or because females have more permission to express their feelings in this society than males?

I addressed myself to the men this time. "Your 'wives' have just described their needs. I'm going to ask you to try to meet those needs. How would you respond to your wife when she says, 'I don't want that person in this house anymore. It's making me very unhappy. Why can't you get rid of her?'"

The men looked at me blankly.

I restated the task: "What might you actually say to your wife to let her know you understood what she was feeling?"

There were some worried stares. Finally one brave soul took the plunge. "I didn't know you felt that way," he ventured.

Another man gained courage. "I didn't know you felt so strongly," he said.

One more man waded in. "I'm beginning to see how rough this whole situation is for you."

I turned toward the women now. "And what might you say to your husband to let him know you understood his feelings about the new husband?"

A hand went up. "It must be very hard for you—having him around all the time."

Another hand: "You take as much time as you want to tell me about what's bothering you."

And finally: "I want to know how you feel . . . because your feelings are very important to me."

There was an audible sigh. A few people applauded. Evidently they liked what they had just heard.

I turned to the father who had had "the emotionalism up to here." "What do you think?" I asked.

He smiled ruefully. "I suppose," he said, "this is your round-about way of telling us that this is what we should be doing for our kids instead of trying to shut them up."

I nodded. "Even as grown-ups who are just pretending," I said, "we can see how comforting it is to have someone who will listen to our negative feelings. Children are no different. They need to be able to air their feelings and wishes about their siblings. Even the unsavory ones."

"Yeah," he said, "but grown-ups have self-control. If you give kids the green light on those feelings, my concern is that they'd start acting them out."

"It's important to make a distinction between allowing feelings and allowing actions," I replied. "We permit children to express all their feelings. We don't permit them to hurt each other. Our job is to show them how to express their anger without doing damage."

I reached for the materials I had mimeographed for the work-shop. "In these pages of cartoons," I said, as I handed them out, "you'll see how all this theory can be put into practice with young children, older children, and teenagers."

INSTEAD OF DISMISSING NEGATIVE FEELINGS ABOUT A SIBLING, ACKNOWLEDGE THE FEELINGS.

Instead of . . .

Put the feelings into words.

Instead of . . .

Put the feelings into words.

Instead of . . .

Put the feelings into words.

GIVE CHILDREN IN FANTASY
WHAT THEY DON'T HAVE IN REALITY.

Instead of . . .

Express what the child might wish.

Instead of . . .

Express what the child might wish.

Instead of . . .

Express what the child might wish.

HELP CHILDREN CHANNEL THEIR HOSTILE FEELINGS INTO SYMBOLIC OR CREATIVE OUTLETS.

Instead of . . .

Encourage creative expression.

Instead of . . .

Encourage creative expression.

Instead of . . .

Encourage creative expression.

STOP HURTFUL BEHAVIOR. SHOW HOW ANGRY FEELINGS CAN BE DISCHARGED SAFELY. REFRAIN FROM ATTACKING THE ATTACKER.

Instead of . . .

Show better ways to express anger.

Instead of . . .

Show better ways to express anger.

Instead of . . .

Show better ways to express anger.

We spent the rest of the evening studying the cartoons, discussing the skills, trying them on for size.

"Maybe when my son complains to me again about how Grandma spends too much time with the baby, I ought to say something like, 'You wish she'd spend more time with you.'"

"The next time Lori tries to hit her brother, I'll tell her to put her anger in her voice instead of her hands."

Everyone was busy trying to figure out how to apply these new skills to the sibling sore spots in their own homes.

At one point I noticed that some people were beginning to look glassy-eyed. It was just as well that our time was up.

As we gathered our belongings to leave, there was an exchange of light banter:

"Who can remember all this stuff?"

"I feel sick. I've said every one of the things you're not supposed to."

"This is too much for me. It'd be easier to send the kids to a therapist once a week."

"Once a week? With what goes on between mine, I'd need a sleep-in therapist."

I listened and thought, "It is unnerving to be in that in-between place where you know what's wrong, but don't quite know how to make it right. No wonder they were all worried.

But having "been there" myself once, I knew that their discomfort was only temporary. With time and practice, and a little success, they'd soon see for themselves that none of these skills was beyond them. They may not have known it, but they were already on their way.

A Quick Reminder . . .

BROTHERS AND SISTERS NEED TO HAVE THEIR FEELINGS ABOUT EACH OTHER ACKNOWLEDGED

Child: I'm gonna kill him! He took my new skates.

With words that identify the feeling
"You sound furious!"

or

With wishes
"You wish he'd ask before using your things."

or

With symbolic or creative activity
"How would you feel about making a 'Private Property' sign and hanging it on your closet door?"

CHILDREN NEED TO HAVE THEIR HURTFUL ACTIONS STOPPED

"Hold it! People are not for hurting!"

AND SHOWN HOW TO DISCHARGE ANGRY FEELINGS ACCEPTABLY

"Tell him *with words* how angry you are. Tell him, 'I don't want my skates used without my permission!' "

The Questions

People came back from this session on acknowledging feelings, filled with questions and eager to share what had happened in their homes. First, their questions.

I tried to show my son that I understood his angry feelings. I even told him, "I know you hate your brother." Yet that just seemed to make him angrier. He screamed, "No I don't!" What am I doing wrong?

Most children experience a mixture of emotions toward their siblings and become uncomfortable or resentful when told they feel only hatred. A more helpful statement would be, "It seems to me that you have two feelings about your brother. Sometimes you like him a lot and sometimes he makes you mad as the dickens."

But what do you do with a child who keeps telling you that he hates his brother? When I answer, "I can hear that you hate him," he shouts back, "Yes I hate him!" I say, "Boy you really do hate him" and he yells, "That's right. I hate him." And we never seem to get anywhere.

In order to help a child stop spinning his wheels in his own fury, it helps to restate his emotions in language that will enable him to move forward. Any of the following might help:

"I can hear how angry you are at David."

"Something he did really bugged you."

"Something he said must have infuriated you!"

"Would you like to tell me more about it?"

I tell my three-year-old, "Don't hit your sister. Go in your room and hit your dolly instead." But she refuses and still goes for the baby. Should I continue using this approach?

There's a difference between sending a child away from you and instructing her to hit her doll, and inviting a child to express her feelings through the use of her doll as you watch. A more helpful statement would be, "I can't let you hurt the baby, but you can show me what you're feeling with your doll."

The key words are "show me." As the child shakes her finger at the doll, or pummels it, the parent can give words to what the child is trying to express.

"You really are annoyed with your sister."

"Sometimes she makes you furious!"

"I'm glad you showed me. If you ever feel that way again, be sure to come and tell me."

I tried having my three-year-old use her doll to show me how she feels about the baby. But when she bashed the doll's head against the floor, I realized that it might be good for her, but I couldn't handle watching it. Am I the only one who feels this way?

You're not alone. Other parents who had similar reactions found that they were much more comfortable about their children using old pillows, clay, finger paints, or crayon and paper as avenues of expression:

"Can you draw me a picture of how you feel?"

"Those black zigzag lines tell me you're feeling fierce!"

"The way you're shaking that pillow shows me you feel, 'Grrrr!!!' "

And if there are no other materials available, we can always use words:

"I can't let you pinch the baby, but you can tell me with words how mad you are. You can say, very loud, 'I'm *MAD!!*' "

I notice that when the relatives visit and fuss over the baby, my five-year-old just wilts. Then later he takes it out on her. Is there anything I can do about it?

Wouldn't it be great if we could just muzzle these well meaning folks? Short of alerting the relatives to the problem ahead of time, you can innoculate your son against some of the pain by bringing out into the open what he's probably feeling:

"I'll bet it can be rough to watch everyone 'goo-goo' over your sister with all that 'Isn't she cute stuff'—even though you know they made the same fuss over you when you were that age. If it happens again, give me a signal, like a wink, and I'll wink back at you. Then you'll know that I know. It'll be our secret."

My son never seems to be able to see things from his sister's point of view. Lately I've been asking him, "How would you like it if she did that to you?" But he never answers me. Why is that?

The question puts him on the spot. Were he to answer you honestly, he'd have to admit that he wouldn't like it. If you want your son to be able to consider another point of view, make a simple statement that gives him credit: "I'm sure you can imagine how that would feel if that were done to you." Now he has to think, "Can I imagine it? What *would* it feel like?" But he doesn't have to answer to anyone except himself. And that's good enough.

My teenage daughter complains constantly about her brother. Sometimes its more than I can take. Do I have to listen to her each time she comes to me?

There will be times for all of us when we will have no tolerance for listening. And it's important for our children to know that. You can tell your daughter, "I hear how upset you are with your brother, but right now it's hard for me to listen. Let's sit down after dinner and talk about it."

One mother who found she had little patience for the steady stream of complaints, bought each of her children a notebook, a personal "gripe-book" to write or draw in when they were mad at each other. The books were put to immediate use, and there was a noticeable reduction in the amount of running to mother.

The Stories

I've been leading groups for many years now, yet I'm always astonished at how parents, after only one or two sessions, are able to go home and put theory into practice, in ways that are both apt and original. Most of the experiences that follow are exactly as they were written or told to the group. A few are slightly edited. Only the children's names have been changed.

The first two stories that came back surprised everyone. They were tales of siblings in utero who were already causing problems.

I'm in my seventh month. When I first told Tara, who's five, that I was going to have a baby, she didn't say anything. But last week she touched my stomach and said, "I hate the baby." I was shocked, but I was glad she brought it up. Because I knew she had to have some feelings of resentment, and if she felt comfortable enough to tell me, it meant she trusted me. But even though I was prepared—almost waiting for it to come—it was like a little bomb.

I said, "I'm glad you told me, Tara. Do you think that maybe with a new baby, Mommy won't have time for you?" She nodded her head. I said, "When you feel like that, come and tell me, and then I'll make time for you."

The bomb diffused and she hasn't brought it up since.

• • •

WHEN MY WIFE and I first told Michael (age six) that his mother was pregnant, he was excited. Then he thought about it for a minute and said, "No way!" That night he started wetting his bed.

After the baby was born, he showed no animosity toward her. In fact he was excellent with her—held her, watched her, was very protective. But with his mother— look out! He tried to kick her . . . hit her. She put a stop to that. She said, "I won't let you hurt me!" Then Michael started smearing things around the house, like toothpaste and vaseline. On top of that we got a call from his teacher. She said he had stopped listening and had a "short attention span."

Kay and I talked it over and we began to think that maybe the reason he was acting this way was because we hadn't ever given him a chance to get his feelings out. I started saying some of the things to him we talked about in class, like "It can make you mad when you see Mommy busy with the baby all the time—nursing her, and changing her." And Kay told him, "Sometimes when a Mommy has a baby, their other children think their Mommy doesn't love them anymore. If you ever think that, you come and tell me right away and I'll give you a special hug." We've also been taking turns giving him time alone—away from the baby.

It has definitely helped. His behavior is much better at home. And at open-school night the teacher said, "I can't believe it. I don't know what's happened to Michael. He's one of my best children now. He is the best reader in his group!"

This next story shows a parent trying to apply her new skills with her ten-year-old son, Hal. Somehow she manages to acknowledge his feelings, even though what he has to say makes her furious.

A few days after last week's workshop, the kids were late coming home from school. So late, that I went out to look for them. There I saw Timmy (six), coming down the road crying uncontrollably. And there was his brother, Hal (ten) walking some distance behind.

I ran to Timmy and he sobbed that Hal had punched him, pushed him down, and kicked him.

I saw red. I wanted to hit Hal, but stopped myself. Instead I held Timmy and tried to comfort him as best I could. When he finally calmed down, I gave him a snack, and he went out to play.

All this time, Hal had been hanging around watching in the background. When Timmy left, he said, "When are you going to hear my side of the story?" I told him, "Now." He then proceeded to tell me how three kids on the bus had threatened to beat him up and how he had dropped his schoolbag and run into the woods to escape them, and how when it was safe to come out of the woods, he saw that Timmy had taken his bag and that he had no right to do that. There was nothing wrong with his having beaten up his brother. Timmy had "asked for it."

Hal was lucky I had been to the workshop. I forced myself to say, "So you feel that because Timmy was carrying your schoolbag home, you were justified in beating him up."

"That's right!" he practically shouted. "It was *my bag!*"

I didn't know where to go from there, so I went into the kitchen to fix supper. After a while Hal followed me and stood silently by me. I looked up and he said in a very low voice, "I want to say something but I can't."

I told him I was ready to listen. He stood there looking very unhappy, unable to say anything. I asked, "Could you write it?"

He got a piece of paper and wrote, "I feel I might have hurt Timmy too much."

I just said, "Oh."

He stood there still looking miserable. I said, "You're feeling really bad about it."

He nodded. Then out spilled all his feelings about

the incident. He was mad . . . the other kids really scared him . . . and finally, "You know, Mommy, if those kids hadn't picked on me, I wouldn't have beaten up Timmy."

I said, "I see."

For the rest of the evening Hal seemed to go out of his way to be nice to Timmy.

One father came up with an entirely original way of acknowledging his daughter's hostility toward her brother. He not only "put her feelings into words," he put her words on paper.

Last night Jill complained bitterly to me about her brother. I tried to tell her I understood, but she was so busy ranting she didn't even hear me. Finally I picked up a pencil and tried to write down what she was saying:

1. Jill objects strongly when Mark picks up extension phone and listens in on her conversations.

2. She hates it when he makes loud chewing noises at the table and scrapes his teeth on fork. Grosses her out.

3. Feels he has no right to come into her room without knocking. Especially objects when she screams at him to get out and he laughs.

When she stopped for breath, I read it all back to her. She was very interested in hearing her own words. I asked her if there was anything else. There was. She added two more grievances which I also wrote down.

Then I said, "Mark's the one who ought to see this list.

But it seems to me, it would be too much for anybody to be hit with five complaints at once. Can you pick out the one or two that bother you the most?"

She read the list over to herself, circled two items, and stuck the paper in her pocket.

I have no idea what happened after that. I'm tempted to ask, but I think I'd better stay out of it.

In their new, experimental frame of mind, parents were eager to see what would happen if they gave their aggrieved children in fantasy what they couldn't give them in reality. The results sometimes surprised them.

Roy (five) came crying to me with a long tale of woe. Billy did this to him and that to him and threw him out of the room and called him a pest.

Mother: That must have hurt your feelings. You wish he'd tell you in a nice way that he wants to be alone.

Roy: (Doesn't say anything, but stops crying.)

Mother: You wish he'd say, "Come on in, Roy. Let's play!"

Roy: Yeah, and he'd let me look in his telescope.

Mother: As long as you wanted.

Roy: And give me some of his stickers. I would do that if I had a little brother.

Mother: You know just the kind of big brother you would be.

Billy: Yeah! (with sudden inspiration) Have a baby!

I couldn't think of anything to say after that.

One of the problems that came right along with learning these new skills was the pressure parents put upon themselves to "do it right" or "say it right" all the time. Happily, they soon discovered that with children you always get a second chance. Here's how one father reversed his direction, right in the middle of an angry confrontation.

Liz's birthday (age eight) caused grumpiness and resentment in Paul (age eleven). He refused to cooperate in any way. When his mother asked him to pick up his own things that were lying around the basement where the party was going to be held, he said, "Get off my case." I was so irritated I told him he was being obnoxious and sent him to his room. He went, and made sure to slam the door with all his might.

I couldn't believe he was behaving so childishly. After all he was eleven years old. Then it occurred to me that even at his age, all the fuss and preparations for Liz might have gotten to him. By the time I went to his room, I was feeling more sympathetic.

I said, "I guess it can get pretty annoying to have to listen to nothing else but 'party, party, party,' all week. Especially when your own birthday is so far away."

"Five months," he said angrily.

I said, "I think it might be six."

He counted on his fingers. "April, May, June, July, September."

"How about August?" I asked.

"Oh no! I forgot about August. Dumb August! That makes it even longer!"

I said, "I bet you wish you could move October up to next month so you could start planning your party right now."

He smiled for the first time that day. Then after a little more conversation in this vein, I left.

A few minutes later he was in the basement whistling and cleaning up for Liz's party.

The idea of channeling the children's negative feelings about each other into some form of creative expression was slow to take hold in the group. One woman told us that the few times she had urged her children to write or draw, they refused. Then someone pointed out that since kids tend to copy their parents' behavior, maybe the next time she was angry at someone, she should sit down in front of the children and draw or write.

She listened politely, but looked dubious. Nevertheless, at the next session she reported what happened when she put the advice into action.

The morning after our last session my T.V. set went completely dead. I called my neighborhood repairman who came right over. In less than ten seconds he had the problem diagnosed. The plug was loose in the socket. He gave it a tap and the set went on. I felt like an idiot.

Then he made out a bill charging me for a full visit, plus tax! I tried to talk him out of it, but he refused to listen. As he walked out the door he called back, "Don't let it aggravate you. It's not worth it!"

I wanted to yell an obscenity after him, but the kids were standing there watching me. I grabbed a big pad and wrote at the top of the page:

I'm **MAD!!!**
I hate that man. He's a robber.
A cheap chiseler.
I'll never use him again.
I'll tell all the neighbors what he did.

Then I drew an "ugly" picture of him with his tongue hanging out and dollar signs for his eyes.

I felt better. I had to laugh at my crude picture. When my husband came home, the kids couldn't wait to tell him what happened.

He was pretty upset at first, but when he saw the picture, he wound up laughing too.

That was the beginning. Since then my kids haven't stopped writing or drawing. Here's what my ten-year-old son typed up about his older brother.

A LIST OF THE FAULTS OF ALEX

1. **Stupidiy**
2. **Dummbness**
3. **Idiosy**
4. **Mentely Retarted**
5. **Teasingly**
6. **Mean**
7. **Bummness**

8.   Queer
9.   Wierd
10. Eggful Onfull

CONCLUSINS

If you meet Alex you will immiditly HATE him
This is classified information

The secret servise

And here's the drawing my daughter handed me one
morning. She said, "Alex broke my red crayon on purpose. This picture shows you how angry I am!"

Two of the parents in our group were coping with an especially difficult problem. Each had a child who was physically attacking and hurting a younger sibling. Although both parents worked at putting all their new skills into action, the one they used most was, "Say it with *words!*"

The words that came out were violent, often horrifying the parent, but the number of attacks decreased dramatically.

I heard the children arguing in Christine's room. Their voices got very loud. Then Hans stormed out of her room and went to his room.

He came back and said to Christine, "You know how mad I am at you? I'm so mad I wish I could poke holes in you just as I'm poking holes in this paper now." (I could hear the pencil ripping through the paper.) "I am not doing it to you. But boy do I wish you were this piece of paper!"

This is such a fantastic improvement in his behavior. Two weeks ago he would have actually hurt her.

• • •

Lori, (age seven) has no control over her temper. Her brother just has to look at her cross-eyed and she'll wham him.

Yesterday I was doing 55 on the thruway, and she started up again.

Lori: (Shrieks) Jason hit me in the eye with his pinwheel!

Jason: I didn't!

Lori: Liar!

Jason: I didn't do it on purpose, I was just making it spin.

In the rearview mirror I see Lori, her fist raised ready to strike.

Me: Oh Lori, that must hurt! A hit in the eye can be painful, even if it is an accident. It can make you angry. Tell Jason how you feel.

Lori called him a long string of names, but at least she kept her hands off him. I was amazed.

Although some parents were impressed by the progress these children were making, others were uncomfortable about one child speaking so menacingly to the other. After some discussion, we concluded that the best way to help a child climb to a higher rung on the ladder of civilized discourse was to model the behavior we wanted. If we were going to insist that children find alternatives to hitting and name calling, then we, ourselves, had to find alternatives. Here's what one Dad did:

I have three teenage daughters and we all do a lot of name calling. My wife and I call them names and they call each other names. What we realized after last week's session is that we've got to cut it out. So the other night, two of the girls were fighting over ice cream and somebody said, "You pig . . ."

I said, "Wait a minute. Mother and I have a new idea. Why don't we all sit down and talk about it."

When we sat down, I said, "You know we're all hurting each other too much with this name calling. We hurt you and you hurt each other, and we're going to try to stop that. Cold turkey."

The reaction wasn't much, just, "Okay Dad, fine . . . we'll stop." But what's good is that we have a process now. Because now when they start fighting and one says, "Get out of my room, jerk," at least I can come in and say, "Hey, one thing we agreed to. There's no more name calling. I'm not doing it and you're not. Tell her what bothers you." And before you know it, there's a dialogue going.

And they do the same to me when I lose my cool. They say, "Dad, I thought you said we weren't going to call names anymore." And I say, "You're right . . . You're right. I'm sorry. I was upset . . . Okay, I don't like it when . . ."

It's a small thing, but it's made a big difference.

The next story was handed in by a mother who used to spank her five-year-old when he teased the baby. This time she tried another approach.

I had had a very bad morning with two cranky children. I returned home from grocery shopping and was relieved to see that the baby had finally fallen asleep in the car. This would give me enough time to unload everything before I fed her her bottle. As I was putting away the groceries, Philip continued to whine and pester. I told him to go outside and make sure that Katie was all right. He was gone too long so I went out to check. The baby was crying and Philip was shaking the rattle in her face. I asked him if he had awakened her and he said yes. He was angry that she was sleeping so long.

It took every bit of my self-control not to smash him. Instead I slammed the car seat with my hand and screamed about how angry I was. Then I picked up the baby and carried her into the house.

Philip would not come in. He locked himself in the car as a self-imposed punishment. I thought, "Good. Let him sit there!"

About ten minutes later, he came in and began telling me that he hated himself. By that time I had cooled off.

"I think we have a problem," I said. "Let's talk about it." We sat down together at the kitchen table. "Sometimes you like the baby and sometimes she makes you angry—very, very angry."

He nodded.

"Let's talk about some ways we can make things better."

Before I could say another word, he blurted out, "Whenever I feel angry, you should keep Katie away from me, because I take all my anger out on her."

I couldn't get over how in touch he was with his feelings. I didn't know a five-year-old could verbalize like that. Since then we've managed to avoid a lot of potential problems. When he's in a bad mood, he'll ask to change seats in the car. Or when Katie is bothering him, I'll suggest he play in another room.

This final incident was told by a woman who usually sat in silence during our meetings. The moment I heard it, I thought of psychologist Dorothy Baruch's persistent theme: Not till the bad feelings come out can the good ones come in.

I always sensed that Melissa (seven) was a little jealous of her sister (three). Not that she's nasty to her. She doesn't hit her or anything. She just sort of ignores her. But it's hard to tell with Melissa. She's not one to talk about what bothers her. She's a lot like me.

Anyway, after last week's session, when the little one was taking a nap, I asked Melissa to come sit on the couch with me. I put my arm around her and said, "I'm glad we can be alone together, because I haven't talked to just *you* in a long time. I've been thinking . . . sometimes it must be a pain in the neck to have a younger sister. You have to share everything with her, your room, your toys—even your mother."

It was like a dam broke loose. She couldn't stop talking, and I couldn't believe what I was hearing. She said such terrible things. How much she hated her! How she wished her dead sometimes. I started to get sick to my stomach. It was a good thing the phone rang, because I don't know how much more I could have listened to.

That night when I went up to check the kids, I thought I wasn't seeing straight. There were the two of them in one bed, sleeping with their arms around each other!

When all of the stories were read or told we looked at each other in wonderment. What a strange and poignant process was going on here. It seemed such a puzzling paradox:

Insisting upon good feelings between the children led to bad feelings.

Acknowledging bad feelings between the children led to good feelings.

A circuitous route to sibling harmony. And yet, the most direct.

THREE

The Perils of Comparisons

So far we had been talking about the fiercely competitive feelings that children bring to the sibling relationship all by themselves, without any help from us grown-ups. I started our third session by asking the group whether they could think of any way in which we adults contributed to the competition.

Someone called out, "We compare!"

No argument there. Everyone seemed to agree that by making comparisons we definitely "heated up" the rivalry. Nevertheless I thought it would be interesting for us to find out what it felt like to be compared, from the child's point of view.

"Be my kids," I said, "and give me your visceral reaction to these statements:

"'Lisa has such beautiful table manners. You'd never catch her eating with her fingers.'

"'How could you leave your report until the last minute? Your brother always gets his work done ahead of time.'

" 'Why don't you keep yourself the way Gary does? He always looks so neat—short hair, shirt tucked in. It's a pleasure to look at him.' "

The feedback was immediate:

"I'm gonna push Gary in the mud."

"I hate his guts."

"You like everybody more than me."

"I can't do anything right."

"You don't love me for me."

"I'll never be what you want me to be, so why try?"

"If I can't be best at being best, I'll be best at being worst."

I was startled by the intensity of the anger and despair I heard in their responses. The last statement in particular jolted me. Do some children make the decision to excel at being bad if they can't excel at being good?

A few people were quick to corroborate this possibility with examples from their personal experience. Then someone reminded us of former president Jimmy Carter and his irrepressible brother, Billy. We all laughed, remembering his antics. Billy was certainly best at being "worst."

One woman shook her head. "It doesn't always work that way," she said. "Some kids don't have that much fight in them. They give up. I know I did. My mother let me know in so many ways how great my sister, Dorothy, was and how inadequate I was compared to her, that I used to wonder why she ever had me in the first place. The best thing I ever did was move a thousand miles away from both of them—my mother and my sister.

"Even now I dread the holidays because my mother can still get to me. She starts right in the minute she sees me: 'Your hair's looking a little dull, dear. Maybe you ought to get it touched up, like Dorothy' . . . 'How are Jennifer and Allen doing in school? Dorothy's children are all in honors classes.' . . . 'Dorothy just got herself a new job at a fabulous salary. That sister of yours is a real go-getter!' It takes me weeks to recover from those visits."

A sympathetic murmur ran through the room. "My father was always comparing my two older brothers," a man said grimly. "Dad died when they were still teenagers, but my brothers have picked up right where my father left off. It's unbelievable. One is 43 now and the other is 47. On one level, they know that what they're doing is ridiculous, but they can't stop. They even compete in terms of their kidney disease. Who is sicker. Who has it worse. Who needs more treatment. Which is the correct treatment modality. Both are on dialysis and each one is trying to prove that his treatment is better. Grown men!"

"Aren't we making a case here?" a woman commented. "These examples are all pretty extreme. I compare my boys from time to time, but I seriously doubt that it's going to do them lasting harm."

The group looked at me.

I looked at her.

"Under what circumstances do you compare?" I asked.

"I don't do it all the time," she said defensively.

"But when?" I persisted.

She thought awhile. "Well, I'm not even sure you could call it comparing. It's more like motivating. For example, I'll say to Zachary, 'Alex gets right down to his homework at night. Daddy and I never have to nag him.' I wouldn't ever say, 'Why can't you *be* like Alex?' "

Dorothy's sister jumped right in. "You don't have to," she said vehemently. "You can be sure Zachary gets the message loud and clear, that his brother is right and he's WRONG."

"But I don't always hold Alex up as the model," the woman protested. "Sometimes I'll praise Zachary by telling him in certain ways he's better than Alex. I'll tell him that he's much handier than his brother, that Alex is all thumbs."

"That's just as bad!" Dorothy's sister exploded. "That's exactly what my mother did to me. I remember the time she told me I was more 'orderly' than Dorothy. It felt great for the moment, but then I began to really worry. Could I keep it up? And even if I could, what would happen if Dorothy ever became 'orderly.' Where would that leave me? I'm sure my mother thought she was giving me a boost, but all she did was make me more competitive with my sister." She paused for a moment, as if debating whether or not to go on. "And more competitive with everyone else," she added. "It took me a year of therapy to realize that as an adult I was still doing to myself what my mother had done to me; and how miserable I was making myself, constantly measuring everything about me against other people. It was so stupid. Because if you look, you'll always find someone who does something better than you. My therapist had a wonderful quote. It was, 'Never compare yourself to others. You'll become either vain or bitter.' Anyway after my experience all I can say is, stay away from comparisons. They can only bring unhappiness."

The woman who had been defending her right to compare, wilted visibly. There was no disputing the conviction behind the words she had just heard. They were spoken with an authority born of pain.

"It's strange," I told the group. "When my kids were young, I swore to myself that I would never compare them. But I did it anyway—over and over again."

People looked at me in surprise.

"I'd hear the words coming out of my mouth," I continued, "and be amazed that it was me speaking. Finally I figured out what was going on. I compared them when I was bursting with anger ('Why do you always have to be the one to keep the whole family waiting? Your brother was in the car ten minutes ago!'). I also compared them when I was bursting with pleasure ('That's terrific! Your big brother has been working on that for an hour, and you figured it out in two minutes!'). In either case, it only led to trouble.

"Here's what helped me break the pattern. Whenever I was tempted to compare one child to another, I would say to myself, 'STOP! DON'T! Whatever you want to tell this child can be said directly, without any reference to his brother. The key word is *describe*. Describe what you see. Or describe what you like. Or describe what you don't like. Or describe what needs to be done. The important thing is to stick with the issue of this one child's behavior. Nothing his brother is or isn't doing has anything to do with him."

I distributed the following illustrations so that the group could see the difference in action.

AVOID FAVORABLE COMPARISONS.

Instead of . . .   Describe what you see or feel.

Instead of . . .   Describe what you see or feel.

Instead of . . .   Describe what you see or feel.

AVOID UNFAVORABLE COMPARISONS.

Instead of . . .

Describe the problem.

Instead of . . .

Describe the problem.

Instead of . . .

Describe the problem.

There were many spontaneous comments as we studied the cartoons together. Most of them centered on the realization that even a favorable comparison could be harmful. Several people said that they could see where this kind of "praise" could give one child a vested interest in keeping the other one down. I was about to move on to the next topic when I noticed a few frowns.

"Something bothers you," I said.

It turned out that there was a great deal that bothered them. I tried to answer their concerns.

"We live in a competitive society. Doesn't a child need competition at home to prepare him to hold his own in the outside world?"

"If by 'holding his own' you mean being able to function competently, assert himself and achieve his goals—all of that can be learned in an environment that encourages cooperation. To me the best part of being raised in a cooperative climate is what comes out of it—more respect for others, more confidence in one's self."

"But isn't there something to be said for competition?"

"Yes, it can also be a spur to accomplishment, but it comes at a price. Studies of people in schools and business settings show that when competition becomes intense, people tend to develop physical symptoms: headaches, stomachaches, backaches. And emotional symptoms. They become more anxious, more suspicious, more hostile. Let our homes be a haven from this kind of stress."

"I never compare, but all I have to do is tell my daughter one nice thing about my son, and she reacts as if I just compared her. She'll say, 'You think he's better than me.' I don't understand her."

"Children often experience praise of a brother or sister as a put-down of themselves. They automatically translate, 'Your brother is so considerate' into 'Mom thinks I'm not.' It's a good idea to save our enthusiastic comments for the ear of the deserving child."

"But what can you do when one child tells you about something special she did and all the others are standing there listening?"

"That's a tough one. We don't want to shortchange the child who is excited about her accomplishment. Yet we do want to be sensitive to the feelings of the others. You'll never go wrong if you describe what you think the child might be feeling ('You must be so proud of yourself!') or what the child has accomplished ('A lot of practice and perseverance went into winning that medal').

"The trick is not to add, 'I'm so thrilled, I can't wait to tell Dad and all the neighbors.' The passion and excitement you feel about a child's achievement should be saved for a moment when just the two of you are together. It's too much for the other siblings to have to listen to."

"But sometimes you can't avoid the other children listening—like at report card time. In my house both kids shove their report cards at me at the same time. Last week my son couldn't wait to show me his B in Math (up from a C last time), and as I was 'oohing and ahhing' over his progress, his sister pointed to her A in Math. Suddenly all the air went out of his balloon. His B no longer had any value."

"You can tell both children firmly, 'There's no report card contest going on here. These are records of your work and behavior in school over the last six weeks. I want to sit down with each of you individually, so I can see what your teacher has to say and hear how you feel about your progress.'"

"But how do I stop the kids from comparing report cards when I'm not around?"

"You can't. And there's no need to. If they want to show each other their report cards, that's their business. What's important is that they know that Mom and Dad see them as separate individuals and are not interested in comparing their grades."

There seemed to be no other questions. I was trying to formulate a summary when I noticed a woman's hand waving at me. As soon as she saw she had my attention, she started right in:

"If my kids only compared grades, I'd be ecstatic. But they compare everything, all day long, down to their belly-buttons. 'Mine's an inny . . . yours is an outty.' And they're always watching and worrying about what the other one has: 'Hers is better . . . his is nicer . . . you bought him that? Why didn't you get one for me?' I find myself constantly trying to equalize. They've got me so worn down that if I buy a pair of socks for Gregory, I'll buy a pair for Dara even if she doesn't need it."

I looked around the room. "Of course," I said, "no one else here has that problem. No one *here* has children who constantly compare and demand equal treatment."

Groans and guffaws.

"Ladies and gentlemen," I announced, "you're about to be relieved of a heavy burden. Next week when we come back, we'll attempt to debunk the myth that children have to be treated equally. In the meantime, see what your efforts not to compare bring you."

A Quick Reminder . . .

RESIST THE URGE TO COMPARE

Instead of comparing one child unfavorably to another, ("Why can't you hang up your clothes like your brother?") speak to the child only about the behavior that displeases you.

Describe what you see
"I see a brand new jacket on the floor."

or

Describe what you feel
"That bothers me."

or

Describe what needs to be done
"This jacket belongs in the closet."

Instead of comparing one child favorably to another. ("You're so much neater than your brother") speak only about the behavior that pleases you.

Describe what you see
"I see you hung up your jacket."

or

Describe what you feel
"I appreciate that. I like seeing our hallway looking neat."

The Stories

The very act of *not comparing* one child to another turned out to be more of a challenge than most people expected. The parents who reported back to the group seemed very pleased with themselves, not only because of what they did do, but because of what they refrained from doing.

> Kay was giving the baby her bottle in the bedroom. I told Michael to come into the kitchen with me and asked him what he wanted for lunch. He started to whine and said, "I don't know what I want . . . I wish I were a baby. Babies get everything done for them. They don't have to get dressed by themselves . . . they don't have to wash themselves . . . they don't have to decide what to eat."
>
> Normally this would have been my cue to launch into a put-down of the baby in order to build Michael up, to say something like, "Yeah, but the baby can't talk or walk and she has to wear diapers." But last week's session was still in my head, so I just tried to show I was listening to *him*. As a result, we had a really nice conversation:
>
> *Dad:* You think that babies have everything done for them and that being a baby is fun.
>
> *Michael:* Yes. Daddy would you like to be a baby or not?
>
> *Dad:* (Joking) I'd like to be an astronaut.
>
> *Michael:* That's not the choice! Would you choose to be a baby or not to be a baby?

Dad: I would choose to be like I am.

Michael: Why?

Dad: I can do more things than a baby. I can make more choices and more decisions.

Michael: You mean if you don't like the color pink, you don't have to wear anything pink?

Dad: Yes.

Michael: Do you like the color blue or green?

Dad: Sometimes I like blue and sometimes I like green. Right now I like blue.

Michael: (Thinking awhile). Right now I want a peanut butter and jelly sandwich!

• • •

JOHN CALLED ME last night from college and sounded happy. He said, "I just got my midterm grades and, of course, it's nothing like what Karen gets, but . . ."

I almost interrupted with my standard, "Well you know how hard she studies and you've always been more interested in sports, so, of course, you can't expect . . . blah, blah, blah."

Then I thought, "No, this time I'll say, 'What has Karen got to do with you? I'm interested in you as *you*, not in relation to your sister.' Then I thought, 'No. Why bring up Karen at all? So I just said, "Paul you sound pretty happy. You must have done okay on your midterms."

Then we talked about his courses and what he plans to take next semester, and we never once mentioned Karen.

• • •

IT'S BEDTIME.

Me: Allen! Jennifer! Bedtime. Pajamas and teeth. (Allen goes off to do it.)

Jennifer: (Whining) No, I don't want to.

Me: Time to get ready for bed.

Jennifer: No, you do it.

Me: (Feeling mad and frustrated and wanting to yell, "Why can't you cooperate the way your brother does?!!!" But I think better of it, and walk into Allen's room to cool down.) Jennifer follows me. Allen's all set for bed.

Me: (To Allen) You're all set. When you heard it was bed-time, you got right into your p.j.'s and brushed your teeth. That was a big help to me. (Notice, not a word about Jennifer.)

BONUS: Jennifer did her things without further ado.
ANOTHER BONUS:

Allen: (From his room) You don't have to worry about getting clothes for me tomorrow. I set them up already. I like being helpful to you.

Me: Thank you, Allen. (To Jennifer) I see that you're ready for bed. (Notice, I didn't say "too.")

Jennifer looks proud.

• • •

MATTHEW (ELEVEN) constantly measures himself against his older brother and comes out "littler" and less able. But last weekend he did something that outshone everyone in the family. Sunday morning our electric lawnmower died. Matthew overheard his father and me moaning about how a new mower would put us even further behind with our bills. A few hours later, he appeared in the driveway with an old fashioned hand mower that he had bought at a garage sale for $3.00 with his own savings.

I couldn't get over it. I was so excited that I almost told him that no one else in the family thought of it. I didn't; his father didn't; and his big brother, who he thought was such a hot shot, certainly didn't. There! That proved he was as good as, if not better than, his brother.

You have no idea how much self-control it took for me just to describe what he did instead. I said, "Matt, you saw how worried Dad and I were about having to buy a new mower; you thought about how you could help us; and you actually managed to find a hand mower that works. And for $3.00!"

Matthew beamed at my description. Then he threw out his chest and said, "I'm a pretty resourceful guy!"

FOUR

Equal Is Less

It was our fourth session.

As I opened the door to our meeting room, I heard peals of laughter. Several women who had arrived early were standing together, evidently sharing something very funny. As soon as they saw me, they waved me over. It seems that they had been discussing the question that had been raised at the end of our last meeting, as to whether or not children should be treated equally, and had come up with some comical examples of what can happen when you're determined to be fair.

Before they could finish telling me about their zany experiences, I interrupted them. "Hold it," I said. "This is much too good for the others to miss." As soon as the whole group was assembled, I asked the women to tell their stories again. Here they are, to the best of my recollection:

Why Isn't There a Roy Goats Gruff?

I was curled up on the sofa with my two boys, Billy and Roy, reading a book we had just taken out of the library. It was the first time they had ever heard the tale of the Billy Goats Gruff and the troll under the bridge. They both loved the story, but when it was over Roy burst into tears. "Why is it all about Billy? Why don't they have a *Roy* Goats Gruff?" he sobbed.

I promised I'd try to find a story with Roy in it, but there was just no consoling him. Can you imagine? I can't even read them a fairy tale without worrying about each boy getting equal billing.

The Haircut

When I was little, I had thin, wispy, brown hair and my sister had a gorgeous gold mane that grew down to her waist. My father was always making a fuss over her hair. He called her his "Rapunzel."

One night while she was sleeping, I took my mother's sewing scissors, tiptoed over to her bed and cut off as much hair as I could without waking her. The next morning when my sister looked in the mirror, she let out a shriek. My mother came running in, took one look at her and became hysterical. I tried to hide, but my mother found me. She screamed at me and hit me. She said my punishment was to stay in my room for the rest of the day and think about what I did. I suppose I was a little sorry, but not too much, because at least now we were equal!

The Haircut II

In my family I was the one with the pretty hair and my mother was the one with the compulsion to make things equal. She was determined that my sister and I be treated exactly alike so that there would be no cause for jealousy between us.

One day she decided that because my sister didn't have curly hair, I shouldn't either. So she took me to the barber and had him cut off all my curls. I looked like a plucked chicken. For the rest of the day I cried and cried and wouldn't talk to anyone. Even now I find it hard to forgive my mother for what she did.

Equal Opportunity Nursing

When my first child was born, I looked forward to nursing her, but was told I couldn't for medical reasons. A few years later when my second daughter came along, I decided not to nurse her either. Not because I couldn't by then, and not because I didn't want to very much, but because I didn't want the first one ever to feel deprived, ever to have to learn that her sister got something she didn't. At the time it seemed to be the only fair thing to do, but now that I look back on it, it seems crazy.

No Amount of Ice Will Suffice

I'll never forget the summer day I decided to tackle the big freezer in the garage and get rid of a two year build-up of frost. The kids were in bathing suits watching me bring out pots of hot water to loosen up the ice. At one point, everything began to melt at once. I playfully tossed a big slab of ice in the direction of one of the kids and said, "Here have some ice." Immediately the other two chimed in, "I want some too."

I grabbed two more big slabs and slid them towards the other two. Then the youngest yelled, "They have more!"

I said, "You want more? Here's more!" and threw a potful of ice at his feet. Then the other two yelled, "Now *he* has more." I threw two more pots of ice in their direction. The first one cried. "Now *they* have more."

By this time, all three children were ankle deep in ice and still yelping for more. As fast as I could I flung huge chunks of ice at everyone's feet. Even though they were hopping up and down in pain from the cold, they continued to scream for more, in a frenzy that one would gain an advantage over the other.

That was when I realized how futile it was to ever try to make things equal. The children could never get enough, and as a mother, I could never give enough.

All the stories were enjoyed, but the last one really hit home. It brought into focus for all of us the sheer insanity of what can happen when kids demand equality and parents feel compelled to deliver it. After a moment's reflection, a father commented, "I can see where you'd wind up doing some pretty weird things when you try to treat everyone the same, but what can you do when the kids start to tighten the screws?"

"Like how?" I asked.

"Like when they bellyache that you're not fair or that you 'gave her more' or 'love him better.'"

"You can tell yourself," I answered, "that even though they seem to want everything the same, they don't really."

He looked at me questioningly.

It was a difficult concept to explain. I told them all the story of the young wife who suddenly turned to her husband and asked, "Who do you love more? Your mother or me?" Had he answered, "I love you both the same," he would have been in big trouble. But instead he said, "My mother is my mother. You're the fascinating, sexy woman I want to spend the rest of my life with."

"To be loved equally," I continued, "is somehow to be loved less. To be loved uniquely—for one's own special self—is to be loved as much as we need to be loved."

There were still a few quizzical expressions.

To help everyone better understand the difference between giving equally with measured amounts, and giving uniquely, in terms of each child's legitimate needs, I handed out the following illustrations:

INSTEAD OF WORRYING ABOUT
GIVING EQUAL AMOUNTS . . .

FOCUS ON EACH CHILD'S INDIVIDUAL NEEDS.

INSTEAD OF CLAIMING EQUAL LOVE . . .

SHOW CHILDREN HOW THEY'RE LOVED UNIQUELY.

EQUAL TIME CAN FEEL LIKE LESS.

GIVE TIME IN TERMS OF NEED.

A few people chuckled appreciatively as they looked through the cartoons. Others seemed upset. A lively discussion ensued, touched off by the group's concerns about what they had just read:

"That situation with the pancakes could have come right out of my house. But what do you do if little Johnny wants more and you're out of the stuff to make it with?"

Two fathers raised their hands.

"How about printing a note with big letters and putting it up on the refrigerator door? BE SURE TO BUY MORE PANCAKE MIX FOR JOHNNY. And then of course, do it."

"How about giving him a bite of your pancake? My kids love getting anything from Daddy's plate. Just yesterday my little girl complained that her brother got more peas, so I said, 'Here have some of mine.' She counted the peas I gave her, put two of them back on my plate, and said, 'Now I give you some of mine.'"

More chuckles.

One woman was irritated. "That's fine if you're in a good mood," she said. "But when I've taken the trouble to cook a good dinner, and the kids start counting and measuring and yapping about who got more, I don't have the patience to be so nice."

"Why worry about being nice?" another man countered. "How about being real? It's very unpleasant to be accused of being unfair. I've told my girls straight out, 'If anybody here feels she doesn't have enough, here's how I like to be asked: "Dad, when you get a chance, can I trouble you for more?"'"

"The problem in my house," another woman said, "isn't with the children. It's with me. I'm the one who feels bad if I don't give them both the same. When I buy something for Gretchen—like new pajamas—and Claudia is standing there watching with a long face, I feel terrible. I never know what to say to her."

"What do you usually say?"

"Oh, I don't know . . . something like, 'But dear, you don't need new pajamas. Yours still fit you.'"

"Sounds perfectly logical to us grown-ups here," I said. "The trouble is, kids don't respond to logic when they're upset. They need some attention for what they're feeling: 'Claudia, it can be hard to watch your sister get new pajamas when you're not. And even though you know all the reasons why she needs them and you don't, it can still bother you.'"

I turned to the rest of the group. "I hope," I said, "that I'm not giving anyone here the impression that we should never give the identical item to each child. There will be times when that will be the obvious and right thing to do. All I want to point out is that if you decide *not* to give equally, for whatever reason, that's all right too. The children who fail to receive won't go under. Your understanding and acceptance of their disappointment will help them to deal with life's inequities."

"That hasn't worked with my older son," a woman said sadly. "I know. I've tried. Maybe it's because in his case there's such extreme inequity. Not with things, but with time. He bitterly resents all the time I have to give his younger brother, who has a learning disability. He even accuses me of liking his brother better."

"You're describing a very difficult situation," I said. "And you're right. Empathy can only go so far toward meeting a child's legitimate needs. I'm wondering . . . do you think it would be at all helpful to your older boy if you were to sit down with him and schedule, in writing, fifteen minutes a day for the two of you to be together—fifteen minutes of private, uninterrupted, phone-off-the-hook time? Or would that be adding another burden on to you?"

She thought a while.

"I don't know," she said. "It might be worth it, because maybe if he knew he could count on the time with me, he wouldn't be so angry anymore. And then maybe it would finally sink in that I don't just prefer his brother, because I really don't!"

"But suppose you did," a man said. "So what? I thought that's one of the things we've been saying here, that we don't have to worry about convincing the kids we love them all equally. It's not even humanly possible to love them the same. I'll bet each person here has a favorite. I'm the first to admit that my boys are good kids, but my daughter is the light of my life."

All my alarms went off. He sounded much too comfortable about a situation that was potentially dangerous. Did he have any idea what pain he could inflict upon all his children with that attitude, including the "light of his life"?

"As I see it," I said, "the problem is not one of having a favorite. We all experience feelings of partiality towards one child or another, at one time or another. The problem is how to make sure we don't show favoritism. We all know that Cain slew Abel when the Lord showed more "respect" for Abel's offering. And we also know that Joseph's brethren threw him into a pit in the wilderness because their father loved Joseph more and gave him a coat of many colors. That was a long time ago, but the feelings that provoked those violent acts are eternal and universal.

"Even here in this room today," I continued, nodding toward the woman who had told the story of "The Haircut," "we heard about a little girl who cut off her sister's hair because her father was enchanted with it."

"Rapunzel's sister" looked at me intently. "The truth is he was enchanted with everything about her. He was never enchanted with me." Her eyes filled. "I can't believe it still hurts," she said.

I wanted to weep for her. And for all the other children who had to watch the glow in their parents' eyes and know that it would never be for them.

"This is going to be a tough one," I said. "How do we protect the other children in the family from our enthusiasm for that one child who speaks to our heart?"

There was a heavy silence. I was surprised. I thought I'd hear at least a few parents protest that the question didn't apply in their case. Not one peep. After several moments of reflection a few people voiced their thoughts.

"I know my son, Paul, is painfully aware of the great pride we take in our daughter. He's told us point blank, 'You and Daddy always look at each other when Liz says something.' At first we didn't know what he was talking about. Then we realized that we constantly exchanged these 'isn't-she-terrific' looks. Since he's alerted us, we've made a real effort not to do it anymore."

"My wife has pointed out to me that when we all take a drive in the car, I tend to ignore the girls. I'll say, 'Mark, look at this . . . Mark, look at that!' I catch myself now and I call out, 'Hey gang, look over there!'"

"I must confess that I've caught myself—more than once—being much tougher on one of my girls than the other. They can both do the same thing at the same time, and I'll come down hard on Jessica, and give Holly a gentle little reprimand. There's something about her that makes me melt. I know I've got to watch it."

"What I hear all of you saying," I said, "is that if we want to stop showing favoritism, we first have to be aware that we feel it.

We need to be honest enough to admit the truth to ourselves. Knowing our bias immediately puts us in a better position to protect our "less favored children"; and it helps us protect our favored child, as well, from the pressure of having to maintain his position and from the inevitable hostility of his siblings."

The woman who had spoken last wasn't satisfied. "What do we do about our guilt?" she asked. "I can admit that I'm partial, but I feel terrible about it."

"Would it help," I answered, "to tell yourself that it isn't necessary to respond to each child with equal passion, and that it's perfectly normal and natural to have different feelings towards different children? The only thing that is necessary is that we take another look at the less favored child, seek out her specialness, then reflect the wonder of it back to her. That's all we can ask of ourselves, and all the children need of us. By valuing and being partial to each child's individuality, we make sure that each of our children feels like a number one child."

There were no more questions.

I looked at my watch. We were five minutes past closing time. People were sitting quietly in their seats, their focus inward. I could almost feel them making connections between what they had just heard and their families. There was no need to give an assignment. They were already in the process of assigning themselves.

A Quick Reminder . . .

CHILDREN DON'T NEED TO BE TREATED EQUALLY.
THEY NEED TO BE TREATED UNIQUELY.

Instead of giving equal amounts
"Here, now you have just as many grapes as your sister."

Give according to individual need
"Do you want a few grapes, or a big bunch?"

Instead of showing equal love
"I love you the same as your sister."

Show the child he or she is loved uniquely
"You are the only 'you' in the whole wide world. No one could ever take your place."

Instead of giving equal time
"After I've spent ten minutes with your sister, I'll spend ten minutes with you."

Give time according to need
"I know I'm spending a lot of time going over your sister's composition. It's important to her. As soon as I'm finished, I want to hear what's important to you."

The Stories

The first story that came back revealed a good deal of soul searching.

> The part of last week's meeting where we talked about playing favorites hit me very hard. It started me thinking about how Jessica (thirteen) must feel about my giving so much time and affection to her sister, Holly (ten). I knew it had to bother her. But it's very difficult for me to be with Jessica. She's so moody. You never know which way the wind is going to blow with her. Everytime we start to have a conversation, we end up fighting. I guess the truth is, I avoid her.
>
> Anyway after the meeting, I began to look for a way that I could be with Jessica peacefully. The next afternoon I stopped what I was doing and sat down on the couch next to her while she was watching her soap opera. I didn't say a word. I just watched with her. The next day I watched with her again. And yesterday she called me in to tell me the show was about to start. We even had a little discussion afterwards about some of the "goings-on." It may not sound like much, but it's the closest we've been in a long time.

The next few stories show parents in the process of redefining their notion of fairness. At first it was hard for them to let go of the old idea that in order to be fair you must give equally in terms of things, amount, time, and even love. Yet, by giving to their children unequally, according to individual need, these parents found a new and liberating way to be fair.

While I was shopping last week, I saw a T-shirt with a unicorn design on it that I knew Gretchen would love. She's crazy about unicorns. I almost didn't buy it because of how her sister, Claudia, might react, but then I thought about our last session and decided to buy it anyway.

When Gretchen opened the bag and held up the shirt, Claudia looked a little taken aback, but she didn't complain.

Then my mother who was watching the proceedings got into the act. She took Claudia aside and whispered, "Never mind sweetheart, I'll buy you a new shirt tomorrow."

"Darn it," I thought, "Claudia wasn't feeling deprived before, but she will if my mother keeps this up."

I put my arm around Claudia and said, "I think Grandma is worried. But we're not. We know that in this family each child gets what's right for her. Sometimes Gretchen will get, and sometimes Claudia will get, but in the end everybody's needs will be met." I couldn't believe what had come out of my mouth.

My mother looked confused. But Claudia and Gretchen seemed to understand.

• • •

UP TILL NOW I wouldn't even consider buying anything for Dara without buying something for Gregory, too. The way they carry on, it isn't worth it. I've been completely intimidated by the two of them.

But yesterday I took the bull by the horns. I bought Data a new lunchbox for school, because she needed it, and came home with nothing for Gregory. The second Dara got into the house, she started, "Nyeh-nyehing" her brother. "Mommy got *me* a new lunchbox and not *you!*"

I shut her up immediately. I said, "I don't like that! That's flaunting. It makes people feel bad. And it makes me sorry I even bought you that lunchbox!" And I was glad Gregory heard me, because he's perfectly capable of doing the same thing to her. They are both going to find out that their mother isn't putting up with that nonsense anymore.

• • •

I HAD TWO incidents this week where I saved a lot of energy by not trying to be fair.

Incident I

It's bedtime.

Stevie: (Age four) Ma, no fair. You were in there with Maggie longer than me. You were talking to her longer.

I was tempted to explain, "Well, your sister had a lot of trouble getting off to sleep tonight. She napped too long. I'll make it up to you tomorrow night. I'll read you an extra story." Instead of all that . . .

Me: Oh you wish I would spend more time with you?

Stevie: Yeah. (And he snuggled right down to sleep.)

Incident II

Stevie wasn't feeling well. I was rocking him on my lap when Maggie (20 months) comes charging up to me, arms up. My first thought was to placate her by putting Stevie down immediately and picking her up. But I didn't. I said, "Maggie, I know you want Mommy to hold you. Right now Stevie needs to be held a long time because he's sick."

Stevie got this "aha" look in his eye, like "See, I'm important!" But what amazed me is that she accepted it and was actually able to wait a half minute until I picked her up.

The next challenge parents faced was to try to liberate their children from their obsession with "equal," "same," and "fair." In these next two examples you'll see how a mother and father joined forces to help their sons get "unhooked" from each other.

The rivalry between our boys reaches a peak at bedtime. Zachary resents having to go to bed a half hour earlier than Alex, just because he's two years younger. Every night it's the same thing. Zachary refuses to settle down. He sings, turns somersaults on the bed, talks to us, talks to Alex even after Alex is in bed, noisily letting him know that he's still up.

This infuriates Alex who feels that his seniority is being challenged. Whenever my husband or I try to be firm with Zachary, he insists that he can't settle down until Alex is in bed.

Earlier this week I got the two of them together to try to talk to them about what each needs at bedtime. It was a disaster. They ended up screaming at each other.

I almost gave up. But the next day I got hold of Zachary alone, and it was a completely different experience. He started by grumbling again that Alex got to go to bed later. But this time I was ready for him. I said, "We're not discussing Alex, we're discussing you."

He said, "But Alex . . ."

I repeated, "He's another subject. I'm not interested in him now. I want to talk about *you*, And what *you* need at bedtime."

That changed the whole direction of the conversation. He told me how hard it was for him to fall asleep. Then I asked whether he could think of anything that might help. He said maybe if he did exercises before bedtime, he'd work off energy. He also said it might help him if he had some quiet time with me or his father before "lights out." So far, this has been working.

• • •

The boys burst in arguing.

Alex: Dad, will you please explain to him that it's all right if he crosses the street when I tell him to. Zachary, that car was a mile away!

Zachary: Yeah, sure, a mile away. I could have gotten killed!

Father: Alex, your timing is just right for you. Zachary, your timing is just right for you. I'm pleased to hear that even though you disagreed strongly with each other, you each trusted your own judgment.

This final story gives us some insight into what our children really want from us, even while they're pressuring us for preferential treatment.

Was I put to the test this week! Amy (eight), my middle daughter, was sitting on the sofa with me and suddenly she asks, "Daddy, who do you love best—Rachel, Emily, or me?"

Everything we talked about last week flew out of my head. All I could think to say was, "Honey, I love you all the same." Brilliant, right?

But she didn't buy it. She said, "Suppose we were all in a row boat, and it tipped over, and everyone was drowning, then who would you save?"

I tried to work my way out of that one. "The one closest to me," I said.

"Suppose they're all the same closeness?"

She really had me on the spot.

Finally, I remembered. "That would be a terrible, terrible situation for me to be in," I said. "Each of you is so special to me, because each of you is so different. What would I do if anything ever happened to my Amy? How could I bear the thought of losing someone who is such a pleasure to be with and talk to? I'd never find another one like her anywhere. She's a complete original. It's torture to even think about it!"

That did it. She seemed completely satisfied. She never even asked me how I felt about her sisters. She just wanted to know how much I valued her.

FIVE

Siblings in Roles

If He's "This,"
Then I'll Be "That"

It was the evening before our next meeting and I could hardly wait. Finally we were ready to tackle the topic that everyone had been waiting for: fighting. We'd spend the whole two hours talking about what to do when the kids go into active combat. With great satisfaction I took one last look at the materials I had prepared, and packed the papers in my briefcase.

The dog banged her nose against my thigh. I ignored her. She barked and butted me again. "Okay, Pepper, okay." I slipped the leash over her outstretched neck and ran up the driveway with her. Two little boys hurried toward us, pointing and squealing, "Doggy! Doggy!"

Close behind them was my new neighbor. The last time I had seen her she was pushing her twins in a stroller. "Barbara!" I exclaimed. "I can't get over how the boys have grown. They're walking and talking now! One thing's for sure, they both like dogs, don't they?"

"Yeah, I suppose . . . But look how the little one is trying to pet her, and notice where the big one is. He can't get far enough away."

I was startled by her comment and not sure how to respond.

"They've been that way from the time they were born," she went on. "The little one is real gutsy. Nothing scares him. But the big one is afraid of his own shadow."

I managed a noncommittal grunt and excused myself, tugging the dog back toward the house. I knew that if I stayed one second longer, I'd say something I'd regret.

How could she talk that way in front of them? Did she think they didn't hear her? Or understand? She had each boy pegged, locked into his role, and was totally oblivious to the damage she was doing—not only to each boy individually, but to their future relationship.

Back inside the house again, I found myself beginning to worry about tomorrow's session. Maybe it was too soon to talk about fighting. Maybe we needed to discuss how casting kids in roles could create the bad feelings that lead to fighting. Otherwise we'd be treating the symptom without understanding one of the major causes. On the other hand everyone was "psyched" for tomorrow's topic, including me. Maybe I should just ask the group to look over the chapters on roles in *Liberated* . . . and *How To Talk* . . . , and let it go at that.

The phone rang. It was my oldest son. He sounded tired.

"Hi Mom. I've been writing term papers all week and thought I'd take a break and call home. How's everybody?"

"Fine. We all miss you. Especially Pepper. She keeps going to your room to look for you."

"It must be hard on her with Andy and me gone."

"I think she mostly misses you."

"Why me?"

"Well, you were the one who took the main responsibility for her."

"That's not true, Mom. Andy fed her every morning."

"I suppose. But you were the one who made sure she had a good run everyday. And nobody but you could clip her nails or clean her ears. Your brother couldn't get within two feet of her with a wash cloth."

"Maybe so," he said uncomfortably. "I don't know . . . Well I'd better get back to work. I've got a lot of reading to do. Say hello to Dad for me."

He hung up.

I couldn't believe what I had done. What could have possessed me? Why did I feel I had to make David the "responsible one?" Why in the world would I encourage him to view himself as being somehow superior to his brother? Was it because I was feeling sorry for him, all alone in that little dormitory room? So sorry that I had to give him a boost at his brother's expense? And I was indignant at what my neighbor was doing to her boys!

That settled it. The workshop on fighting would have to wait. Tomorrow we were going to talk about roles, but in a new way. We needed more understanding of what lay behind our impulse to cast our children into roles. We needed to explore, not only how a given role affects each child individually, but how each child's role affects the other siblings, and ultimately their relationship with each other.

• • •

IT WAS THE FOLLOWING EVENING. I waited impatiently for people to take their seats.

"Fighting tonight?" a woman asked hopefully as she slid into her seat.

"Next week," I answered. Then I told them—about my neighbor, my phone call, my thoughts.

They listened soberly.

"Now here's what I'd like to know from you," I said. "What do you think it is that drives some parents to assign different roles to their children? I've already mentioned one possible cause— the misguided need to bolster a child's ego—even at his sibling's expense. What else?"

Their answers came quickly:

"The misguided need to bolster our own egos. My guess is that your neighbor was a timid little girl when she was growing up, and that's why she bragged about having a 'gutsy kid.'"

"And the opposite is true, too. I think we tend to project our own weaknesses onto our children. I know I'm always accusing my son of being a 'procrastinator,' yet I'm the world's champion at putting things off."

"Also I think we sort of enjoy the idea that we've got each kid figured out. Sometimes I'll call my son 'Punctual Paul' or tease my daughter for being a 'Late Lizzie.' It's kind of a family joke."

"I think we put our children in different roles because we want each of them to feel special. I don't know if it's the right thing to do, but I tell my three, 'You're good in reading; your sister is good in math; and your brother is good in art.' It's a way of giving each of them a separate identity."

Suddenly a hand shot up. "I just realized something," a woman exclaimed. "Parents aren't the only ones who put their kids in roles. *Kids put themselves in roles, too!*"

The group quickly shifted gears and pursued her thought.

"It's true. A kid will play the 'good boy' part because it brings him love and approval."

"Or the 'bad boy' part because it's a way of getting attention, even negative attention."

"Also children are smart. They know there are payoffs that come with certain roles. The 'clown' in the family can get away with murder. The child who plays 'helpless' has everyone doing things for him."

The same woman waved her hand again. "And we haven't even mentioned the fact that *kids push each other into roles!* And that has nothing to do with the parents either!"

I asked her to explain.

She thought a moment. "I'll give you an example from my own home. My oldest boy, who's small and skinny, is always bragging about how strong he is and calling his younger brother a 'weak wimp.' And the younger one, who's built like a Mack truck actually believes him. He thinks of himself as weak and he acts that way. Anything you ask him to lift or carry is 'too heavy.' He has no idea of his own strength. And if his older brother has his way, he'll never find out."

We sat there, overwhelmed by the size and complexity of what we were up against: We put the children in roles. The children put themselves in roles. The children put each other in roles.

A man raised his hand. "May I play devil's advocate for a moment?"

We all turned to look at him.

"If it's such a natural thing for children in a family to be cast into roles, then maybe there's a good reason for it that nobody's mentioned yet."

"Like what?" I asked.

"Like, let's say you've got a child who you praise for being the family brain. Wouldn't that child tend to study harder, and do better in school and ultimately better in life? What I'm saying is, there could be advantages to being put in a role."

Three irate people started to talk at once. "You first," I said, pointing to the woman whose face had turned beet-red.

"Sure there are advantages for the privileged child," she said scornfully. "It's great for him. But how about the others? They automatically become second rate."

The next woman jumped right in. "And look at the hostility that's created when one child is put above the other. My brother was the family beauty. People would always come up to my mother and gush, 'Your son is absolutely gorgeous! He looks like Robert Redford! . . . And oh, so this is your daughter. Isn't she sweet.'

"At the time I thought it didn't bother me. But I want you to know that I've had a recurring dream for years now where my brother and I are walking down a street and suddenly his face gets caught in a giant nutcracker."

Gasps and laughter.

After the group quieted down, the third woman had her say. "I can tell you from experience that it's no picnic for the child who's been given the privileged role either. It's a lot of pressure. My parents always praised me for being the most 'responsible one,' and I lived up to their expectations. But it came at a price. To this day, my brother and sister still play helpless, and I'm stuck with all the family problems."

Now almost every hand in the group was raised. Everyone wanted to tell about the roles they were cast in as they were growing up and how it affected them. Each account, though completely different, had the same pattern. One role seemed to determine the other: "I was always the slob; my brother was Mr. Clean." . . . "I was the holy terror; my sister was little goody two-shoes."

And once the drama was cast, the characters seemed to play out their parts almost compulsively: "I decided that if I was always being accused of being 'wild,' I might as well *be* 'wild.' " . . . "Since people expected me to be sloppy, I wouldn't disappoint them."

And always the antagonism that resulted between brothers and sisters: "I resented my brother for being the 'capable one.' Next to him I felt inadequate." . . . "I hated my sister for having a terrible temper. It forced me to be the calm one."

And even if the roles were not direct opposites, the children were defined—or defined themselves—in terms of the other: "I wasn't as popular as my sister." . . . "I wasn't a leader like my brother."

And always ending with the sad sound of "to this day." "To this day there's tension between us." . . . "To this day we can't seem to relate." . . . "To this day I feel something is wrong if I'm not being the funny one . . . the neat one . . . the responsible one."

When the last experience had been shared, we were all quiet, reflecting upon what we had just heard. Someone asked, "Isn't it possible to have a family where each sibling's role somehow meshes smoothly with the others, and the whole family functions as one harmonious unit?"

"I suppose so," I answered, "but we also need to prepare our children for life outside the family. And life demands that we assume many roles. We need to know how to care for and be cared for; how to be leaders and followers; how to be serious and a little 'wild'; how to live with disorder and how to create order. Why limit any of our children? Why not encourage all of them to take chances, explore their potential, discover strengths they never dreamed lay within them."

Our devil's advocate was not impressed by my fine speech. "You're talking about some kind of ideal," he said. "Let's face it. People have natural abilities and natural limitations. My older daughter is a gifted musician. She's ten and already playing the entire Haydn Concerto in D. The younger one has a tin ear, so we've steered her towards gymnastics."

He could not have chosen a worse example to make his point with me. His words triggered the memory of a part of my childhood that I hadn't thought about in years. The experience was back with me now, fresh and raw as ever. I told him the whole story, from the very beginning: about the new mahogany piano that my parents proudly bought for the children; about watching my big sister play and longing for the day when I would be old enough to take lessons; about my first year of actual lessons with a teacher who was constantly telling me that I was his "worst pupil"; and how, despite his criticism and my ineptitude, I happily played my few simple pieces for hours on end; and finally, about the big consultation between my parents as to whether or not it "paid" to continue my lessons.

I knew the verdict before it came. My sister was "the musician." Maybe they could find something else for me. I accepted their decision without protest. They were right. Hard as I tried, I seemed to learn slowly and with great difficulty.

But the loss of the music was a terrible loss for me. Only as the months went by did I realize how much I missed it. I couldn't bear to listen to my sister play. Every note hurt.

Furtively, when no one was around I would take out my old books and try to teach myself. I even made some progress. But in the end, the task overwhelmed me and I gave up. Music was not to be for me.

The man stared at me. He looked as if he were about to say something when a woman spoke in a tremulous voice "My parents gave me piano lessons when I was eight. My little sister used to watch me practice, and when I finished she would sit down at the piano and try to copy me. Then one day she went to the piano, and, without a single lesson, played the piece I had been struggling to learn for over a month. After that I stopped practicing. I told my mother I didn't want lessons anymore."

"And your mother let you stop?" I asked.

She nodded.

"I wonder, how would it have been, if instead of accepting your decision, your mother had said, 'I see no reason to quit. You seem to be enjoying the piano and you're making progress.' How would you have responded to that?" I asked.

"I probably would have said, 'But you're wasting your money. Ruth plays better. She knows my whole piece already.'"

I continued speaking as her mother: "Honey, I can see how that could be discouraging, but Ruth's playing has nothing to do with you. Whether someone learns a piece quickly or slowly isn't important. What's important is the meaning *you* bring to the music that no one else will. What's important is the pleasure you get from playing. I wouldn't ever want you to deprive yourself of that."

She held back her tears. "That would have meant everything to me," she said.

"I know," I said. (Oh boy, did I know!) "There are a lot of little boys and girls out there who are being cheated of their rightful opportunities because of a sibling's special prowess."

I addressed the whole group now. "It's true, there are children who do have great natural gifts, and those gifts should certainly be recognized and encouraged. But not at the expense of the other siblings. When one child stakes out his or her area of special competence, let's be on guard about excluding the others from that area. And let's make sure that the others don't exclude themselves. Let's be wary of statements like, 'He's the musician in the family' . . . 'She's the scholar' . . . 'He's the athlete' . . . 'She's the artist.' No child should be allowed to corner the market on any area of human endeavor. We want to make it clear to each of our children that the joys of scholarship, dance, drama, poetry, sport are for everyone and not reserved for those who have a special aptitude."

There wasn't a murmur of opposition.

"Suppose we use this next week," I said to everyone, "to see whether any of our children is playing a role, for whatever reason, and to think about how we might free that child to become his most whole self."

Suddenly I remembered. "Oh no!" I exclaimed. "I've completely forgotten. I promised you all a session on fighting next week!"

My "devil's advocate" gestured to me reassuringly. "It's okay," he said. "So they'll fight for one more week. This is important."

Freeing Children to Change

The beginning of parent meetings are usually slow. People need time, after a busy week of outside activity, to reconnect with the concerns of the group.

Not this bunch. They picked up the thread of last week's discussion as if they had just returned from a coffee break.

"I thought a lot about your assignment last week and decided that nobody in my family puts anybody in a role. Then on Sunday I introduced my boys to the new minister and heard myself say, 'This is my oldest, this is my middle and this is my baby.' I didn't even mention their names! And I have to admit, that's how I treat them. I spoil my five-year-old because he's the youngest; my middle one is just there, sort of sandwiched in between; and I'm always after the ten-year-old to 'act his age.' "

"I know what you mean," a father said. "Ever since Kay had the baby, I find myself pushing Michael to act more grown up. Last night I told him he was a big boy now and should get into his pajamas by himself. He looked unhappy. He said, 'Daddy, don't you realize that under this skin I'm still very little?' "

"That's the one thing we didn't mention last week," someone said. "And it's so obvious. We do treat the children according to their birth order."

"And sometimes," another woman said, "we treat them according to *our* birth order."

We looked at her in total confusion.

"I'll try to make it short," she said. "I was an older sister who always considered my little brother a big pest. As a result, I get very uptight whenever I see my son bothering his older sister and right away accuse him of being a 'pest.' I guess I identify with my daughter.

"Now my husband, who was a younger brother, has the opposite reaction. He identifies with my son, sees him as the victim, and is always accusing my daughter of being 'mean' to her little brother. So in my husband's script it's our daughter who is the 'oppressor' and our son who is the 'oppressed.' "

The problem intrigued us all. A few people confessed that they, too, tended to identify with the child whose role corresponded most closely to their own as they were growing up. But others were quick to point out that you didn't need a particular past history to see one child as oppressed and the other as the oppressor. They told about having children who really were passive and gentle, and others who really were "meanies," "little rats," "bullies."

"Could someone give me an example?" I asked.

"My two girls," a woman said. "I know it's hard to believe, but it's the three-year-old who's the bully. She'll grab things from her older sister, scratch her, bite her . . . and her sister just sits there like a schnook and takes it. She won't even try to defend herself. It kills me to see it, but I never know what to do."

"What do you do?" I asked.

She laughed with embarrassment. "Probably all the wrong things," she said. "I tell the little one she's being bad, and make her leave the room."

"And what's so infuriating," I added, "is that an hour later she's back doing it again."

"Exactly!" the woman exclaimed. "Only usually it's a minute later. But what else can I do? I have to stop her, don't I?"

"Absolutely. But the idea is to stop her in a way that doesn't reinforce each girl's role."

To make the situation she described more vivid for everyone, I asked the woman to pretend to be her own three-year-old. I would be the mother. Would someone volunteer to be the older sister? Someone did. We played the scene twice. The first time I gave all my attention to the three-year-old "aggressor" and ignored her sister. The second time, I gave my attention to the older sister. Here's what we enacted.

DON'T GIVE YOUR ATTENTION TO THE AGGRESSOR.

ATTEND TO THE INJURED PARTY INSTEAD.

The woman who had played her own three-year-old was amazed. "What a contrast!" she said. "The first time, when you yelled at me and shook me, I thought, 'This is great. I've really got Mommy now!' But the second time, when you paid all that attention to my sister, I thought, 'It ain't worth it. I'm not gonna do that again!'"

"But suppose you've got the kids pegged wrong?" another woman said. "My sister used to hit me all the time so my mother thought she was the bully. What my mother didn't know was that I teased my sister on purpose to *make* her hit me, so I could get her into trouble. My mother never caught on."

Wicked little grins on quite a few faces. Evidently this sibling scenario was not uncommon.

"That's another good reason," I said, "*not* to cast our children into roles. Even as firsthand observers of the action, we could easily arrive at the wrong conclusion."

The mother with the two daughters shook her head. "That may be so," she said, "but in my opinion, each child is born with a certain nature, and nothing you do as a parent is going to change that. I know my two were different right from birth. They were like night and day. The younger one was always a little stinker, and the older one . . ."

I had stopped listening. I knew exactly what she was going to say. What's more, at one time I would have agreed with her completely. I sighed inwardly. How do I get through to her? Briefly I considered telling about my own boys, but decided against it. That was one memory I didn't want to revive.

The room suddenly seemed airless. The woman continued to hold forth about the immutability of personality traits. Finally she arrived at her conclusion: "So it's like hitting your head against a stone wall to think you're going to change human nature."

I looked around the room hoping to find a champion for another point of view. There were none. Just a bunch of people sitting there looking resigned. I thought, "Well, that's it. Here goes.

"I used to feel as you did," I said slowly, "especially when my children were young. I had decided that my oldest son was a born bully, and my youngest boy was innately sweet and gentle. And every day there was fresh evidence that I was right, because every day David seemed meaner and meaner, and every day Andy seemed more vulnerable, more pathetic, more in need of my protection.

"The turning point came when the boys were about ten and seven. I was in a session with Dr. Ginott and heard him say something about treating our children, not as they are, but as we hoped they would become. That thought revolutionized my thinking. It freed me to look at my boys with new eyes. What *did* I hope them to become?

"The answer didn't come easily. I had to do a lot of talking to myself: 'Sure David could be mean and aggressive, but he was also capable of being kind, of using restraint, of getting what he wanted in ways that were peaceful. Those were the qualities in him that needed to be affirmed.'

"At the same time I knew I had to stop thinking of Andy as a 'victim'—to get rid of that label in my own head. I said to myself, 'There is no victim in my house anymore. There's only a boy who needs to learn how to protect himself and demand respect.'

"The very act of changing my thinking wrought miracles. Anyway it seemed like a miracle to me when I saw how the boys responded to my new expectations. Part of that story is documented in *Liberated Parents/Liberated Children*. But what I didn't write about is what I'm going to tell you now." I took a deep breath. I had no taste for dredging up this next part.

"It was a Saturday morning. The boys were fooling around in the kitchen. I was making breakfast, feeling great, congratulating myself on how well they were getting along. Out of the corner of my eye I saw David holding a tablespoon over the electric coil from which I had just removed a pot of boiling water. Suddenly he said to Andy, 'Want to see how hot it gets? C'mere.' When Andy got close, David grabbed him and pressed the red hot spoon onto the bare skin of Andy's neck.

"Andy screamed in pain. I screamed. David ran out of the room. I took care of the burn as best I could, and tried to comfort Andy. Then I went into the bedroom and sat down.

"I don't think I'd ever been so depressed in my whole life. What David had done was so cold, so cruel, so calculating, so deliberately vicious, I felt like a fool to have trusted him. He'd never change, no matter how I saw him. He was born with an evil streak. He was a bad seed. He was no part of me.

"Then I heard a knock on the door. It was David.

"I could hardly summon up my voice. 'What do you want?' I asked.

"He didn't answer. He just came in and stood there, looking small and scared.

"Something turned inside me. I don't know where it came from, but I heard myself saying, 'Boy, was that a dumb thing to do! Dumb! Dumb! Dumb! You remind me of your Uncle Stu.'

" 'Uncle Stu?' "

" 'Yeah, your beloved Uncle Stu. The one who takes you fishing and who's such a great guy. Well as his kid sister I can tell you he wasn't so great to me. Once he ripped my torn toenail off my big toe, and it bled and hurt like hell, and he made me promise not to tell my mother.'

"David was stunned. 'Why did he do it?'

"'Because when kids are growing up, they experiment and do crazy, dopey, cruel things to each other. But it doesn't mean that they're crazy or cruel.'"

"David's whole being changed before me. He had done something monstrous, thoroughly reprehensible, but if his mother didn't see him as a monster, and if his uncle who had done something so mean turned out all right, then maybe there was hope for him, too.

"After David left I sat on the bed, turning the whole scene over in my mind, again and again. Suddenly it came to me that just thinking of David another way was only part of the answer. The rest of the answer lay in demanding that he *behave* differently, and holding him accountable for behaving differently. That's what he needed from the grown-ups in his life.

"A week later he tested me again. He was following his brother around the living room, teasing him to tears. But this time I didn't despair. Instead I took him by his shoulders, spun him around, and fixed my eyes upon him. 'David,' I said fiercely, 'you have a superior capacity to be nice. *Use it!*'

"He grinned sheepishly. But the teasing stopped."

Everyone in the group seemed fascinated by my story. "I'm impressed," someone said. It was the woman who had been making the case for nature over nurture.

I addressed her directly. "The point you made earlier is true: Children are born with different personality traits. But as parents we have the power to influence those traits, to give nature a helping hand. Let's use our power wisely. Let's not place our children in roles that will defeat them."

The woman looked troubled. "But I wouldn't even know where to begin," she said. "How would I go about it? I mean if I were going to make the kind of changes with my two that you made with your boys, I'd need more to go on."

A father said, "I'm beginning to see that this is a complicated thing. If you're going to help one child change, you've got to be prepared to work on the others, too."

I had an idea: "Why don't we take an example of two children in the same family who are playing out opposite roles, and see if we can figure out how to get them both unstuck from those roles?"

"Okay," he said.

"What shall we use as our example?" I asked.

He didn't hesitate. "How about the one you were just talking about—where one child is a bully and the other is a victim? Because that's what I have with my son and daughter . . . if that's agreeable to everyone else here."

It was more than agreeable to everyone. Evidently, the bully/victim combination was a popular one.

I thought about how to structure our exercise and decided that since we had concluded last week that a child's role in the family came primarily from three sources—parents, the other siblings, and the child himself—it might make sense for us to isolate a moment when each of these sources was doing its damage, and then see what, if anything, we could do about it. Our task would be two-fold: to free the bully to be compassionate; to free the victim to be strong.

Here's what we worked out in cartoon form.

NO MORE BULLIES.

Instead of the parent treating the child as a "bully" . . .

The parent can help him see that he's capable of being civil.

When the other siblings treat him as a "bully" . . .

The parents can give the siblings a new view of their brother.

When the child sees himself as a "bully" . . .

The parent can help him see his capacity for kindness.

NO MORE VICTIMS.

Instead of the parent treating the child as a "vicim" . . .

When the other siblings treat her as a "victim" . . .

When the child sees herself as a "victim" . . .

The parent can show her how to stand up for herself.

The parents can give the siblings a new view of their sister.

The parent can help her see her potential strength.

A Quick Reminder . . .

LET NO ONE LOCK A CHILD INTO A ROLE

Not his parents
Instead of: Johnny, did you hide your brother's ball? Why are you always so mean?
Parent: Your brother wants his ball back.

Not the child himself
Johnny: I know I'm mean.
Parent: You're also capable of being kind.

Not his brothers or sisters
Sister: Johnny, you're mean! Daddy, he won't lend me his scotch tape.
Parent: Try asking him differently. You may be surprised at how generous he can be.

If Johnny Attacks his Brother, Attend to the Brother
Without Attacking Johnny
Parent: That must hurt. Let me rub it. Johnny needs to learn how to express his feelings with words, not fists!

We were pleased with the examples we had worked out, but were also surprised at how long it had taken us. It took some thought to figure out a statement that would help both children view themselves differently.

I looked at my watch. We had a half hour left to go. It seemed to me that we had already explored our subject in depth and that this might be a good time to consolidate our thinking. I handed out copies of the "quick reminder" sheet I had prepared at home and told everyone to stretch their legs and take a five minute break.

No More Problem Children

The room emptied out. Some headed for the water fountain, others stood around in the hallway talking. I sat at my desk and looked over my notes to see where we would go next. Actually we had covered all the main points and a good deal more. I considered dismissing the group early.

Suddenly I realized that I wasn't alone. A woman was standing in front of my desk waiting for me to look up. She seemed agitated. "Can I talk to you privately?" she whispered.

I motioned to her to sit down.

"I'm very upset by this whole discussion," she said speaking rapidly. "The implication is that any child can be freed from playing any role. But that simply isn't so. What about the child who is afflicted with a serious problem or handicap? The handicap, itself, becomes a role, and no one can free a child from that."

I wasn't sure what she was getting at.

"And it's no one's fault," she went on, her voice quavering. "It's not the parent's fault. I didn't give my son a learning disability. It's not something his siblings have done to him. And he certainly hasn't done it to himself. Nevertheless, he's stuck in his role and nothing anyone does is going to change that!"

This was a big one. There would be no early dismissal tonight.

"Please," I urged. "The point you make is important for us all to think about. Would you consider sharing your thoughts with the group?"

"I don't think they'd . . . I'm probably the only one here who has a . . . well, if you want me to."

When we all reassembled, she repeated to the group essentially what she had told me.

They listened thoughtfully and then delicately pressed her for more details.

"Well," she said reluctantly. "Whenever Neil doesn't understand something, he throws himself around, kicks, curses, makes weird noises, and then he'll talk about how dumb he is. He sees himself as learning disabled. That's his role. And that's what he acts out all day long."

People shifted uneasily in their seats. I was uneasy too. I should have trusted this woman's instincts not to reveal her painful situation to people who couldn't possibly understand her experience. Everyone here had normal kids with normal problems.

Another woman raised her hand and spoke with slow deliberation. "What you describe is very familiar to me. My son, Jonathan, has cerebral palsy, and no matter how much we try to help him, he's constantly frustrated by what he can't do. He's always angry—at me, his father, his sister, but most of all at himself. I would say his identity is very much tied up with his cerebral palsy."

The group was hushed. Stymied. The problems presented by these mothers seemed too extreme to yield to any of the skills we talked about here.

Very gently, someone asked Jonathan's mother, "How does your daughter react to all this?"

"Oh, Jennifer is wonderful, just wonderful! She makes very few demands upon me."

Almost everyone looked relieved. Except one man. He was scowling.

"I'm sure she is wonderful," he snapped, "but she shouldn't have to worry about being wonderful. It's not fair to her. She's a kid. She should feel free to make demands. She shouldn't have to tiptoe through her childhood in order to compensate for her brother's problem."

Several people looked at him in dismay, startled by the harshness of his words. He ignored them and continued addressing himself to Jonathan's mother. "I'm speaking from experience," he said. "My younger brother was a sickly child. When he was seven he had asthma; when he was thirteen he developed ulcers. All my parents ever thought about or talked about were Donald's illnesses. 'Donald's asthma is better today' . . . 'Donald's ulcers are worse today.' What I needed wasn't important. I'll never forget the time I was fourteen and I asked my father for money to go to the movies. He was furious with me. He said, 'How could you even think about going to the movies when your brother is so sick!' "

Jonathan's mother was visibly distressed.

"Look," he continued, "I'm not minimizing what you're going through, but take it from someone who has been one of those 'wonderful' kids. It's a lousy role. It's a big pressure to have to be wonderful all the time. Kids deserve the right to be ordinary—and to have their ordinary needs be just as important as the child with the problem."

"I grew up with a sister who was handicapped," another

woman said bitterly, "and I know exactly what you're talking about."

Her comment took me by surprise. Evidently more than one person here had firsthand experience with siblings with serious problems.

"My parents," the woman continued, "made me feel that since I was 'normal,' I didn't deserve attention. But my sister was waited on hand and foot because she was in a wheelchair. I always sensed that she acted more helpless than she was, and took advantage. If I ever asked for anything, my mother and grandmother would say, 'You should be ashamed of yourself. Your sister needs so much more than you.' And then they wondered why I wasn't nice to her!"

"Well," I said slowly, trying to absorb what I had just heard, "it would certainly seem that when one child is viewed as the 'problem child' for whatever reason, certain dynamics go into motion:

- The problem child becomes more of a problem.
- The burdened parent begins to make demands upon the 'normal' children to compensate for the problem child.
- The needs of the normal siblings are brushed aside.
- The normal siblings begin to resent the problem child.

"How in the world," I continued, "do you have a good relationship with a sibling you resent, and probably feel guilty about resenting?"

"You don't," the man said. "That's just the point."

My brain went blank. "Then what do you see as the solution?" I asked.

He answered forcefully. "Exactly what we've been saying here all along: Don't put children in roles. See them as whole people. Why should it be any different with a child who's handicapped or sickly? My brother Donald was more than just his asthma or his ulcers."

The woman whose sister was in a wheelchair spoke with equal fervor: "I would say, treat all of the kids as if they're okay people. Even the kids with the serious problems. They can do a lot more than we give them credit for."

Their voices rang with conviction. The theory was beautiful. But was it practical? Was it realistic to think that we could treat children as if they were basically capable, basically okay, especially when they were right in the middle of exhibiting their "problem" behavior? It seemed a tremendous challenge.

"Let's see if it can be done," I said to the group. "Let's take the same situations you mentioned earlier—the child with cerebral palsy screaming in frustration, the child who is feeling defeated by his learning disability, the child in a wheelchair who is acting more helpless than she is—and see whether we can, at these trying moments, treat all the children in the family as if they're all 'okay.'"

After much discussion, here's what we worked out:

NO MORE PROBLEM CHILDREN.
INSTEAD OF FOCUSING ON CHILDREN'S DISABILITIES,
FOCUS ON THEIR ABILITIES.

Instead of . . .

Encourage ability.

Instead of . . .

Encourage ability.

Instead of . . .

Encourage ability.

From all our work and all our discussion, a new conviction began to emerge within the group. Several people struggled to put it into words, each building upon the thoughts of the others:

"What I'm seeing now is that it's up to the parent to set the tone, to make it clear that no one in the family is 'the problem.'"

"Some of us might have greater needs or greater challenges, but we all need to be accepted as we are."

"And each of us is capable of growth and change."

"Which doesn't mean we won't have problems, but we'll deal with each problem as it comes up. The important thing is to believe in ourselves."

"And believe in each other."

"And support each other, like a team. Because that's what being a family is all about."

My eyes swept across the room. I could almost see the resolve forming on people's faces. A big seed had been planted during this meeting, and I wondered what would come of it.

A Quick Reminder . . .

CHILDREN WITH PROBLEMS DO NOT NEED TO BE VIEWED AS PROBLEM CHILDREN.

They do need:

Acceptance of their frustration:
"This isn't easy. It can be frustrating."

Appreciation for what they have accomplished, however imperfect:
"You got a lot closer that time."

Help in focusing on solutions:
"This is tough. What do you do in a case like this?"

The Stories

The seed took. The single idea that we, as parents, have it within our power to help free our children from the prison of their rigid roles stirred everyone's imagination. Suddenly there was no limit to what a child could become. Group members reported that the moment they made an inner decision to view their children with fresh eyes, some unlikely events took place in their homes:

From the time Claudia was a little girl, she was "organized." She was the kind of child who, without a word from anyone, would pick up her blocks and put them away—in size order, no less. Gretchen, on the other hand, is a complete scatterbrain. She never puts anything away and never knows where anything is. So this weekend when I noticed that my pantry was a total disgusting wreck, I almost automatically said, "Come on, Claudia, you're my organizer. This is a job for you."

But I didn't. Instead I went to Gretchen and said, "Gretchen, I can't stand it. We've got to do something with this pantry. Can you help me out?"

She said, "Okay," and then she took everything out of the pantry: boxes, bags, jars, cans, utensils. I got so nervous because I thought, "She'll never get that mess back in, and I'll have to end up doing it."

But this kid not only stuck with it, she didn't quit until every shelf was scrubbed down and everything was put back in perfect order. She even found a place for my grocery bags in a drawer, so I ended up with more room than I had before.

Can you believe it? My disorganized, scatterbrained little nut (only kidding) did a beautiful job!

• • •

WE THOUGHT we were doing Michael a big favor by always telling him how "grown-up" he was. It was, "Mommy, Daddy, our *big* boy and baby." But after last week Kay and I had a long talk and decided that we've been depriving Michael of his baby part. For instance when the baby started to crawl, we said, "Hey, look at her go!" and made a big fuss over her. When Michael started to crawl around the floor after her, we stopped him and told him that was no way for a big boy to behave.

So we went on a campaign. The first thing we did was give up the labels altogether. No more "big boy" and "baby." Now it's Michael and Julie. And I think it's helped. Yesterday I had Julie on one knee, and Michael climbed up on the other. He began bouncing up and down and said, "I'm Superbaby!" Then he looked at me to see how I'd react. I smiled and said, "Hi Superbaby!" Since then his favorite game is to sit on my lap and play Superbaby who came home from the hospital walking, talking, running and swimming!

• • •

THIS IS my first attempt at helping Hal (the bully) and Timmy (the weakling) see themselves differently.

I hear noises in the bedroom I don't like. I investigate and find Hal, grinning, sitting on top of Timmy who's pinned to the floor. I'm about to yell, "Hal, get off him! *Now,* you big lummox, before you kill him!" But then I remember.

Me: (Trying to sound casual) Well Timmy, it's a good thing you have a brother who can teach you how to rough-house without being too rough. (Hal looks amazed)

Me: And Timmy, it's a good thing you're tough and can take it. (Now Timmy looks amazed)

I leave the room and pray.

For the next few minutes I hear THUD, BANG, but no screams. Then Timmy comes into the kitchen in tears. Hal is right behind him.

Timmy: He hurt me!

Me: (Not sure I can keep this up) Tell Hal. Then he'll know not to use so much force.

Timmy: I did!

Me: Tell him again. Tell him you won't wrestle with him if he won't listen to you. *He has to agree to let up when you say it hurts.* Hal isn't stupid. He can understand that.

They look at each other and run back to the bedroom. A few seconds later I heard a piercing scream. I race toward the bedroom. Before I reach the door, I hear . . .

Hal: I'm sorry. I said I'm sorry! Punch me back. Ow! Not so hard. Come on, I'll show you how to do a hammerlock.

More thuds. then CRASH!
I open the door. The bookcase is knocked over and all the games and books are spilled all over the floor.

Me: Now, I'm mad!! You are *both* in big trouble with me! Don't you dare to show your faces until this entire room is put back in order!

They giggle guiltily and start picking up books. For the first time they're on the same team—partners in crime.

I leave the room with an angry frown, but inside, I'm one big smile!

Once parents became aware of how their words and attitudes could lock a child into a role, they also became more alert to what the siblings said to and about each other. Whereas before this session they might have ignored one child stereotyping another, now they refused to let it pass. Here are some excerpts of dialogue from written stories.

Billy: (To me in front of his brother, Roy) I'm not like Roy. He's shy. I say hello to people.

Mother: Sounds as if you like being able to say hello to people. When Roy decides he wants to say hello, he will too.

• • •

Alex: Mom, Zachary is such a picky eater. He wouldn't even taste the tuna fish.

Mom: Zach knows what he likes. He'll try it when he's ready.

• • •

Philip: (To his baby sister) Bad girl!

Father: Hey, I don't like to hear any of my children called "bad." If you don't want Katy to chew on your teddy bear, then give her one of her teething toys.

• • •

Karen: Ma, I lost my lunch money.

Sister: Again?

Karen: It's not my fault. My pocket had a hole in it.

Sister: You're so careless.

Mother: That's not how I see you, Karen. I think you just
need to find a safe place to keep your money.

Finally, as parents became convinced that seeing any one child
in a negative role ultimately harmed the relationships between
all the children, they renewed their efforts to bring to light what
was positive about each child and positive about themselves as a
family.

My youngest daughter, Rachel, has always been on the
clingy side—even more so now that her mother and I are
divorced. Her sisters only make things worse by calling
her a "pesty baby" and a "nuisance."
    I was wondering what I could do about it when I
suddenly remembered an exercise I had done in a human
relations class in college, called "Strength Bombardment."
We each had to write down three things we liked about
the other students, and I'll never forget how terrific it felt
when I saw the list of things people had written about me.
    So the next time the girls had their weekend with me,
I told them all to take pillows and sit on the floor in the
living room. Then I explained that we were going to be
doing something special tonight. Each of us would have

a turn to say three things we liked about the others, and I would write down what they said, on a separate paper for each girl. I told them we'd start with Rachel.

Amy said, "Rachel's nice."

I said, "The idea is to tell something in particular that you like about Rachel." Amy came up with, "I like the way Rachel comes into the room and laughs and tells me about a funny show she's watching."

Rachel started to smile.

"One more," I said.

"I like the way Rachel asks me to read to her."

I went on to collect six more comments about Rachel. Then we went on to "do" the other girls. The comments became more and more specific. They said things like,

Emily: I like Amy's imagination when she's playing with dolls and makes up sensible sentences with them.

Amy: I like Emily's manners like, "Pass the potatoes please."

Rachel: I like the way Emily comes in my room when I feel bad, and says, "What's the matter, Rachel?" and she puts her arm around me.

The more we went on, the more enthusiastic they became about each other. Then Amy asked, "Could we also say things we like about ourselves?"

I said, "Sure," and then I added more things to each girls' list.

Amy: When a stray cat is frightened, I can talk quietly to her and soothe her.

Emily: I like the way I teach Rachel to play games.

Rachel: I like the way I comb my own hair.

Nobody picked on Rachel for the rest of the weekend, and I noticed that before they left each girl made sure to pack her list in her overnight bag.

• • •

WHEN JONATHAN (four and a half) was a baby, we discovered that he had C.P. (Ataxia). We knew we would all have many adjustments to make, but surprisingly one of the hardest for us was giving up our outdoorsy lifestyle. Up until then we had been an athletic family. Bill and I love backpacking and Jennifer, my eight-year-old, is a super athlete. She has wonderful coordination and balance. She ice skates, plays tennis, swims and is the fastest runner in her grade school.

Jennifer would beg us both to take her skating on weekends, and one of us usually would, but it meant the other had to stay home with Jonathan. We tried to explain to Jen that her brother couldn't do regular activities, but she always complained that he "ruined everything."

Well after this last session, it came to me that I was doing the wrong thing to both Jon and Jen by constantly focusing on what he couldn't do and asking her to understand that her brother wasn't normal. On Saturday morning we held a family meeting, and I told everyone that from now on our family would create what for us would be a "new normal." From this day forward our life would be different from other families, but it would be *our* normal. Each family member would be accepted as is, totally, unconditionally. Each person would take part or not take part in family projects or outings and sports as he or she wished or at his or her own level. Then we all got dressed to go skating.

Jennifer was the first one on the ice. She skated off, fast as the wind and oh so gracefully. Then Jonathan stepped onto the ice—outfitted with rented skates, a helmet, a pillow in front, a pillow in back (tied around him with Daddy's belt) and two adults to hold him up—one on each side.

It took us fifteen minutes to skate around the rink with Jon, but he was thrilled. Jen whizzed by us about twenty times shouting encouragement to her brother. As we stepped off the ice Jon flashed us an ear to ear grin and said, "Boy, I bet you didn't think I could skate that well!"

SIX

When the Kids Fight

How to Intervene Helpfully

Finally. Fighting.

"Is this really it?" a woman asked. "No more postponements? Because I've been waiting for this moment since our first meeting."

"Don't tell me your children are still fighting with each other!" I said in mock horror.

She was in no mood for joking. "Not nearly as much," she said earnestly. "I'm doing a lot of things differently and they're definitely getting along better. But whenever they do fight, I still have trouble handling it."

"What are we usually told to do when the kids fight?" I asked the group.

"Stay out of it," several people answered almost in unison.

"What else?"

"Let them work it out themselves."

"Why?"

"Because once you start interfering, the kids will always want to involve you."

"And, if you always settle their arguments for them, they'll never learn to settle things themselves."

"So," I said, "you all seem to agree that it's a good idea, whenever possible, to ignore the bickering and tell yourselves that the children are having an experience in handling their disagreements."

The woman who had opened our session was not satisfied with my summary. "I'm not talking about a little bickering," she said. "I'm talking about screaming and cursing and throwing things. I can't ignore that."

"That's exactly what we'll be discussing tonight," I said, "how to intervene helpfully in the children's fights when we feel we must. But first I think it's important to take a moment to ask ourselves whether there might be any reasons for the fighting that we haven't mentioned until now."

I had posed the question to a group of experts. Their answers came in rapid succession:

"My daughter fights over property—whatever she has is hers, and whatever her brother has *should* be hers."

"Mine fights over territory—'Daddeeeee, he put his foot in *my room!*'"

"I know I used to fight with my sister to get my father to take my side, to prove that he loved me better."

"This may sound far out, but I think sometimes siblings of the opposite sex will start a fight as a way of dealing with sexual feelings they might have for each other. It's one way to maintain a safe distance."

Several people raised their eyebrows, but no one disagreed. The list continued to grow:

"Sometimes kids pick a fight because they're mad at themselves and have no one else to let it out on."

"Or because they're mad at a friend and can't punch him so they punch a brother."

"Or because a teacher yelled at them at school."

"Or because they have nothing better to do. It's that way with my son and his little sister. He devils her out of boredom. He says, 'Do you know your legs are going to fall off? . . . Do you know when you were born you were a puppy?'"

"My son starts up with his little brother so he can feel like a big shot. Once while he was teasing him, I said, sort of sarcastically, 'Boy, it's fun to bug your brother, isn't it?' And he answered, 'Yeah. It gives me power. I need it for my soccer game.'"

"My kids fight because they love to see the show I put on. Two minutes after I get them into bed, I hear 'Maaaaaaah, he's jumping on me! . . . Maaaaaaah! He's in my room!' I come running up the stairs yelling, 'What's going on? Stop it! Stop it! Stop it!' It went on like that for weeks before I found out what was happening. They finally admitted to me that they were banging on the wall between them and pretending they were fighting. It was all made up to get me up there six times a night. They thought that was terrific."

A few laughs, a few grunts, a few sighs.

"It's nothing to laugh at in my house," said the woman who had opened our discussion. "Some of the things my boys do frighten me to death. The other day they were throwing heavy wooden blocks at each other. After I broke up the fight and sent them to their rooms, I had such a headache I had to lie down. Then as I was stretched out on the bed with a washrag on my head, I heard the two of them laughing and starting to play with each other. I thought, 'Wonderful for them! I'm glad they're over it. I've got a migraine.'"

"That's one headache we can do something about," I said. "Suppose we start by examining how we usually react when the kids fight." I asked for two volunteers—one to be a big brother and one to be his younger sister.

"That's me," a man said getting out of his seat.

"And me," said a young woman stepping forward. "I'm still the kid sister in my family."

I spoke to the "big brother" first. "You're about eight years old. It's been a long, rainy morning, and you're looking for something to do. Suddenly your eyes light upon your old blocks and a set of toy animals. (I handed him a bag of blocks and another of plastic animals.) It's mostly stuff for little kids, but you've got an idea! You're going to make a zoo, maybe with a jungle for the monkeys and a pool for the seals . . . There are all kinds of possibilities."

The man playing the older brother sat on the floor and began to line up his animals and erect a structure. As he was building, I took the "kid sister" aside and whispered to her. "You don't have anything to do this morning either. You haven't played with those boring old blocks or animals in a long time, but when you see your brother looking as if he's having so much fun, you plop down beside him and say, 'I wanna play too.'"

I went back to my seat and we all waited to see what would happen next.

The fireworks started almost immediately:

Sister: I wanna play too.

Brother: No. I'm making a zoo and I want to do it myself.

Sister: (Grabbing zebra and two blocks) I can play too if I want to.

Brother: No you can't. Give it back!

Sister: Yes I can. It's mine!

Brother: I had it first!

Sister: I can have it if I want to. Daddy gave it to me too.

Brother: (Grabbing her hand and forcing her fingers open) Give!

Sister: Ouch! You're hurting me!

Brother: I said Give!!

Sister: Maaaaaaah, he's hurting me! Make him stop! Mommeeeeee!

I turned to the parents. "At a moment like this, what do you usually do? Don't censor yourself. Just tell us the first thing that comes to mind."

"I'd run in and tell them to stop."

"I'd take the toys away and send them both to their rooms."

"I'd tell them they were behaving like animals."

"I'd try to convince them to play nicely and to share."

"I'd get to the bottom of it and find out who started it."

"I'd take the big one's side. He had it first."

"I'd stick up for the little one, and tell the big one to find something else to play with."

"I'd tell them their fighting was making me sick."

"I'd tell them that I didn't care who started it, I just want it ended."

I said, "We have a rare opportunity. I'd like you to repeat what you've just said to these 'pretend children' so that you can hear for yourself how your words affect them."

One at a time each parent walked over to the quibbling siblings and made his "pitch" to stop the fighting. After each statement, the "children" gave their reactions. Here, in cartoon form, is what happened (you'll see the same Dad trying one approach after the other):

UNHELPFUL RESPONSES TO KIDS WHO ARE FIGHTING.

UNHELPFUL RESPONSES TO KIDS WHO ARE FIGHTING.

By the time we came to the end of the exercise, it was painfully clear to everyone that the standard strategies for coping with kids' quarrels only led to more frustration and resentment between them.

Then I set out to demonstrate yet another approach a parent could take. First I described the steps I planned to keep in mind as I waded into the fight:

1. Start by acknowledging the children's anger towards each other. That alone should help calm them.

2. Listen to each child's side with respect.

3. Show appreciation for the difficulty of the problem.

4. Express faith in their ability to work out a mutually agreeable solution.

5. Leave the room.

Here again, using the same cartoon figures, is what happened when I tried to put each step into action:

HOW TO RESPOND HELPFULLY
TO KIDS WHO ARE FIGHTING.

KIDS WORKING IT OUT.

When our exercise was over, I asked the "children" to tell me more about their reactions to my intervention.

> *Brother:* I felt you respected me and that you had confidence in me. I also liked that you said the solution had to be fair to each of us. That meant I didn't have to give in.

> *Sister:* I felt very grown up. But it was a good thing you left the room, because if you hadn't, I might have put on a show for you and started to scream again.

Now it was the group's turn to ask questions of me.

"But suppose the kids don't have the foggiest idea about how to work it out? My two would just stare at each other."

"In that case you could casually offer a simple suggestion or two before you leave. Like, 'You might want to take turns. . . . Or play with the things together. Talk it over. You'll know.'"

"But what if they try to work it out and go back to screaming at each other? What then?"

I spoke to the "pretend children" again as their mother. "I'm going to do something," I said, "that one of you may not like. *I'm* going to decide who gets what. Brother, you can continue making your zoo. Sis, you come with me and keep me company. But after dinner tonight, all of us need to have a talk. We need to work out some rules for what to do when one person is playing with something, and the other person wants to play too.'"

The next comment came from the woman with the migraine. "But we still haven't dealt with the question of what to do when the kids are in real danger of being hurt by each other."

"We'll deal with it right now," I said. "You walk into the room and find your younger boy standing on a chair, threatening to throw a metal truck at his brother. And the older one is menacing the younger one with a baseball bat." "That's it!" she exclaimed. "That could easily happen with my kids."

"Unfortunately," I said, "it *did* happen with mine, and the drawings I'm about to distribute now illustrate the skills that saved my life and my boys' lives on more than one occasion."

Every hand was stretched out for my handout.

WHEN THE FIGHTING IS HEADING TOWARD HURTING.

1. DESCRIBE

2. ESTABLISH LIMITS

3. SEPARATE THEM.

"What I liked about these skills," I said, "was the power I experienced as I used them. My loud, forceful description of what I saw them about to do stunned them and stopped them. My strong conviction that *no hurting would be allowed in our home* overrode their rage at each other. And in the end I saw that they were grateful to have a parent who cared enough about them to protect them from each other."

"Your kids were lucky," a man said ruefully. "My twin brother literally tyrannized me when I was growing up, and my parents were oblivious. They could look right into their own living room, and see me being beaten up, and not even react or know it. To them it was just 'kids fights.' I always wondered, 'How could they let him get away with it? Why couldn't they have stopped him?' Here were these big powerful parents. You figure they could sit this kid down and make him know that under no conditions could he use me as a human punching bag. But somehow it was never done, or at least never in such a way that it ever had any effect upon him."

"Is it possible," another man asked, "that your parents didn't realize what was going on? Maybe they thought you were just horsing around. I know with my guys, it's sometimes a fine line between roughhousing and the real thing. And I'm not always sure which is which."

"If you're not sure," I said, "it's a good idea to ask the children outright, 'Is this a play fight, or a real fight?' Sometimes they'll answer, 'It's a play fight,' and two minutes later you'll hear crying. That's your cue to return and say, 'I can see this has turned into a real fight with real hurting, and *that* I won't permit. It's time to separate.'"

"But what if one of them says, 'It's a play fight,' and the other says, 'No it isn't. It's a real fight! He *hurt* me.'"

"That's your opportunity," I answered, "to establish another 'rule of the house.' *Play fighting only by mutual consent.* If someone isn't enjoying the roughhousing, then it has to stop. It's important to establish the value that one child should not be taking his pleasure at the expense of the other."

"I wish my mother and father had known that," a woman said. "The most devastating memory of my childhood was of my brothers holding me down and giving me what they called the 'tickle torture.' They made me laugh until I could hardly breathe. And my parents let them. They thought everyone was having fun. Neither one of them thought to ask if it was okay with me."

"I'm getting a little confused," another father said. "At the beginning of this session, we agreed that it was important to stay out of the kids' fights. But all I've been hearing since then is that we ought to intervene. I feel as if I'm getting two different messages."

"Both messages have their place," I said. "Children should have the freedom to resolve their own differences. Children are also entitled to adult intervention when necessary. If one child is being abused by the other, either physically or verbally, we've got to step in. If there's a problem that's disrupting the entire household, we've got to step in. If there's a problem that keeps coming up that hasn't yielded to their solutions, we've got to step in.

"But here's the difference: We intervene, not for the purpose of settling their argument or making a judgment, but to open the blocked channels of communication so that they can go back to dealing with each other."

"But what if they can't?" he asked.

"That can happen," I said. "There are some problems which are so emotionally charged that the children aren't able to work them out on their own. They'll need the presence of an impartial adult. And that's what we'll be talking about next week—how we can help our children with the tough problems.

"In the meantime you've got a lot of new skills to try out, and I'm sure your children will supply you with many opportunities for practice."

"Wait, you'll see," a woman said, "This week, just to spite me, they won't fight."

Her husband leaned over and patted her reassuringly. "With our kids, honey, you have nothing to worry about."

A Quick Reminder . . .

HOW TO HANDLE THE FIGHTING

• •

Level I: Normal Bickering.
1. Ignore it. Think about your next vacation.
2. Tell yourself the children are having an important experience in conflict resolution.

Level II: Situation Heating up. Adult Intervention Might Be Helpful

1. Acknowledge their anger.
"You two sound mad at each other!"

2. Reflect each child's point of view.
"So Sara, you want to keep on holding the puppy, because he's just settled down in your arms. And you Billy, feel you're entitled to a turn too."

3. Describe the problem with respect.
"That's a tough one: Two children and only one puppy."

4. Express confidence in the children's ability to find their own solution.
"I have confidence that you two can work out a solution that's fair to each of you . . . and fair to the puppy."

5. Leave the room.

Level III: Situation Possibly Dangerous.

1. Inquire:
"Is this a play fight or a real fight?" (Play fights are permitted. Real fights are not.)

2. Let the children know:
"Play fighting by mutual consent only." (If it's not fun for both, it's got to stop.)

3. Respect your feelings:
"You may be playing, but it's too rough for me. You need to find another activity."

Level IV: Situation Definitely Dangerous! Adult Intervention Necessary.

1. Describe what you see.
"I see two very angry children who are about to hurt each other."

2. Separate the children.
"It's not safe to be together. We must have a cooling-off period. Quick, you to your room, and you to yours!"

How to Step In So We
Can Step Out

We had a little trouble getting the next session off the ground. Some people were bursting to tell how differently they had handled their children's fights. Others wanted to pick up from where we had left off last week.

Tension between the two opposing camps.

A father grinned and yelled, "Fight! Fight!"

Another pounded on the desk and shouted, "I wanna tell . . . I wanna tell *now!*"

I played along. "Some of you can't wait to tell everyone how effectively you used your new skills last week."

"Right!" he shouted.

"And some of you," I said, turning to the others, "are impatient to get on with more instruction. You don't want to hear stories. You want more information about how to cope with the fighting!"

A chorus of "Yeahs!" and laughter.

"What do we do in a case this?" I asked.

There was general good-natured agreement that we should be "grown-up," and defer our gratification. We would tackle the hard problems first and leave twenty minutes at the end of the session for the stories.

"Last week," I began, "the point was made that some children might have differences between them which are too difficult for them to resolve by themselves. Yet our tendency as adults is to make light of our children's quarrels, to dismiss them as just 'kid stuff,' and hope that they'll somehow blow over. But it's important for us to be aware that some of the problems between brothers and sisters don't 'blow over.' They persist and become a major source of stress and concern to the children.

"How do I know? Because youngsters I've interviewed have told me plainly how unhappy they were because of what their siblings were doing to them."

I picked up my notebook and turned to the list I had compiled. "Here are just a few examples, in their own words, of what the children had to say:

'My older sister yells at me all the time like she's my mother.'

'My brother always sits around while I do all the work. He says it's my job because I'm a girl.'

'My brother says I sing terrible and won't ever let me sing around the house.'

'My sister bugs me till I hit her, then I get into trouble.'

'My brother is mean to my pets. He picks up my gerbils by the tail and drops them.'

'When my parents go out, my brother bosses me around and hurts me if I don't do what he says.'

"When I asked these children if they had ever tried to tell their parents what bothered them, the answer, in every case, was either, 'They won't listen to me' or 'They say I'm being dramatic' or 'They tell me to work it out with my brother.'"

I put my notebook down and looked up into some very worried faces.

A long discussion ensued. We asked ourselves some hard questions: How could we get past our initial resistance to taking the children seriously? How could we make it possible for us to listen to them, and for them to listen to each other?

Here's the procedure we finally agreed upon (we used as our example the case of the girl who complained that her brother bossed her around and hurt her when her parents weren't home):

Helping Children Resolve a Difficult Conflict

1. **Call a meeting of the concerned parties and explain the purpose of the meeting.**

   "There's a situation in this family that's causing unhappiness. We need to see what can be worked out to help everyone feel better."

2. **Explain the ground rules to everyone.**

   "We're calling this meeting because something is bothering Janie. First we'll be hearing from Janie—with no interruptions. When she's finished, we want to hear how you see things, Bill, and no one will interrupt you."

3. **Write down each child's feelings and concerns. Read them aloud to both children to be sure you've understood them correctly.**

   "It scares Janie when we go out. She says Bill is mean to her. Last time he turned off the TV and yanked her off the couch and hurt her arm."

"Bill says he only turned off the TV because she was watching too long and wouldn't listen to him. He feels he pulled her arm gently and couldn't possibly have hurt her."

4. **Allow each child time for rebuttal**

   Janie: I have a black and blue mark to prove you hurt me. And my program had only five minutes to go!

   Bill: That's an *old* black and blue mark. And the program was just beginning.

5. **Invite everyone to suggest as many solutions as possible. Write down all ideas without evaluating. Let the kids go first.**

   Bill: Janie should listen to me because I'm older.

   Janie: Bill shouldn't be allowed to tell me what to do or hurt me.

   Parent: Hire a sitter.

   Bill: Let me go out.

   Janie: Let me have a friend over.

   Bill: Before Mom and Dad leave, set up a schedule for TV and bedtime.

   Janie: People should be their own bosses and in charge of themselves.

6. **Decide upon the solutions you can all live with.**

No sitter.
No hurting.
No bosses.
TV schedule to be worked out in advance with parents.
Each person to be responsible for self.

7. Follow-up

"We'll meet again next Sunday to see if we're satisfied with the way things are going."

• • •

During our entire discussion a man was glowering and mumbling to himself. When we finished our task, I signaled to him that the floor was now his.

"As far as I'm concerned," he announced, "this whole 'format' is too 'nicey-nice.' If my son had done that to my daughter, he never would have gotten off that easy. I would've told him, in no uncertain terms, 'If I hear once more that you've laid a finger on your sister while we're out, you're going to have to deal with me buddy.' He made a fist. 'And that ain't gonna be fun!'"

A few people called out in approval: "Hear! Hear!" . . . "You tell him!" . . . "Get tough!"

Then came the counterreaction:

"That might make *you* feel better, but it could put your daughter in more danger from your son. Because he'll find some way to get even with her."

"Not only that, but what have you taught him? He learns to rely on his father for discipline, instead of himself."

"And how come you're so ready to take your daughter's word over your son's? Maybe *she's* the one who is lying."

The man opened his mouth to reply, thought better of it, and fell silent.

Another father picked up the cudgels. "I don't see why every argument between the kids has to turn into a long problem-solving session. In my opinion there's a time and place for a parent to step in and take over, even if it means taking sides."

"Like when?" I asked.

"Like when one kid is being completely unreasonable."

"For instance?"

"Well, like last Sunday. We were all getting ready to go on a bike trip, and I overheard my son pleading with my daughter to lend him her old knapsack. She flat out refused. Said he'd 'ruin it.' Ruin it? That's a joke. The thing is ready for the garbage which is why we bought her a new one in the first place. I got so mad, I yelled in, 'Give that knapsack to your brother, *now!*'"

"Did she?" I asked.

"You better believe it. I let her know if she didn't, she could stay home."

"How did she react to that?"

"She sulked for a while. But so what? She learned that in a family you've got to share."

"That wouldn't teach me to share!" a woman said indignantly. "I'd be furious if my father did that to me. Things aren't just things. They're like part of you; they're connected to memories. I have an old moth-eaten sweater in my closet that I haven't worn in years, but I wouldn't lend it to anyone—especially not my sister. If I had been the parent in your house, I definitely would have sided with your daughter."

"So," I said, "we have two opposing points of view:

1. Take the side of the child who owns the knapsack.

2. Take the side of the child who needs the knapsack."

I began to distribute the materials I had planned for this meeting. "The first page of cartoons," I said, "shows two sisters fighting—not over a knapsack—but over a blouse. The next page shows what happens when the parent hands down the final decision, either in favor of the property owner or in favor of the 'have-not.' Finally, on the last page you'll see what happens when a parent gives support to one side by stating a rule or value, but leaves the final decision up to the children."

A BATTLE OVER PROPERTY.

WHAT HAPPENS WHEN THE PARENT
HANDS DOWN THE FINAL DECISION.

IN FAVOR OF THE PROPERTY OWNER.

IN FAVOR OF THE "HAVE-NOT"

WHAT HAPPENS WHEN A PARENT SUPPORTS ONE SIDE, BUT LEAVES THE FINAL DECISION UP TO THE CHILDREN.

Boy, you two sound pretty upset with each other.

I need the blouse for the class party, and it doesn't even fit her anymore!

I see. So you wanted to wear it to the party.

But Ma, it's my favorite blouse!

It's still special to you even though you've outgrown it.

Well, it's your blouse and your decision. But if you want to work something out with your sister, that would be between the two of you.

I'll trade you. You can wear my new silver earrings all week, if I can wear your blouse just for today.

Well... I don't know... Okay, but don't spill anything on it.

Gee thanks! I'll be real careful.

I gave the group a few minutes to look over the cartoons and then addressed the father who made his daughter give up her knapsack. "What do you think about all this?" I asked.

He hesitated. "Well, in a way the mother was still taking sides. She told the oldest daughter that she didn't have to lend her blouse. In essence she was saying, 'Don't share.' I don't see what's so great about that."

Two hands shot up.

"She wasn't saying, 'Don't share.' She was making it clear that property rights must be respected. That's a principle that protects both children."

"And by protecting the rights of the older girl, the mother made it possible for her to even consider lending her blouse to her sister."

The father shook his head in disgust. "I still don't see what's so terrible about kids being taught to share. But I'm obviously not getting through," he muttered.

"You're getting through to me," I said. "And I feel you're making an important point. Children should be encouraged to share, and for very practical reasons. Just to get along in this world, they'll need to know how to share—goods, space, themselves. And for spiritual reasons as well. We want our children to experience the pleasure and goodwill that comes from voluntary giving. *Making* children share, however, only makes them clutch their possessions more tightly. Forced sharing undermines goodwill.

"Let's get back to the purpose of this session and the purpose of this course. We are searching for ways to increase good feelings between our children. For ways to make fighting less likely. When parents take the stance: 'In this house *I'm* the one who's going to decide who has to share, who gets to keep; what's reasonable, what's unreasonable; who is right, who is wrong,' the children end up becoming more dependent upon the parent and more hostile towards their siblings.

"What eases the tension, what makes harmony possible, is the attitude of 'Who needs what? . . . Who feels what? . . . What solutions can be worked out that take everyone's feelings and needs into account?' We're not so much interested in technicalities as we are in each other's well being.

"We haven't got all the answers yet. All we have is a direction. Basically we try not to interfere, but when we must step in, it's always with the thought that at the earliest possible moment we want to turn the children back to dealing with each other. That's the best preparation we can give them for the rest of their lives."

I glanced up at the clock at the back of the room. There were only a few minutes left to the session.

"Well folks," I said, "it doesn't look as if we've left ourselves much time for stories."

"What stories?" a woman said. "Oh yeah, the ones on fighting we were going to save for the end. That's okay. They'll keep till next week. I have a question I've been wanting to ask for a long time."

Other hands went up.

"Me too. What do you do when . . ."

"I've been wondering about . . ."

This group was indefatigable. The subject, inexhaustible. The only thing that seemed to be coming to an end was me.

"Please," I said, "will those of you who have questions, write them down while I pack up. I'll take them home with me and give you all copies of my written answers next week. In the meantime, be sure to pick up your reminder sheets."

A Quick Reminder . . .

WHEN THE CHILDREN CAN'T WORK OUT A PROBLEM BY THEMSELVES

1. Call a meeting of the antagonists. Explain the purpose and the ground rules.

2. Write down each child's feelings and concerns, and read them aloud.

3. Allow time for rebuttal.

4. Invite everyone to come up with solutions. Write down all ideas without evaluating.

5. Decide upon the solutions you all can live with.

6. Follow-up.

A Quick Reminder . . .

HOW TO GIVE SUPPORT TO THE CHILD WHO ASKS FOR IT WITHOUT TAKING SIDES

Jimmy: Daddy, I can't finish my map for school. Make her give me the crayons!
Amy: No. I have to color my flower.

1. State each child's case.
"Let me get this straight. Jimmy, you need the crayons to finish your homework. And Amy, you want to finish coloring."

2. State the value or rule.
"Homework assignments get top priority."

3. Leave the doorway open for the possibility of negotiation.
"But Jimmy, if you want to work something out with your sister, that's up to you."

4. Leave.

The Questions

It's the day before our final session. It occurs to me that I had better get around to looking at the questions people had left on my desk. I leaf through the pile and it comes home to me again that this subject is truly inexhaustible. The more one knows, the more one wants to know. Here's what people asked and here are my answers.

Aside from not forcing sharing, how else could you encourage it?

1. By putting the children in charge of the sharing. ("Kids, I bought one bottle of bubble soap for everyone. What's the best way to share it?")

2. By pointing out the advantages of sharing. ("If you give her half of your red crayon, and she gives you half of her blue crayon, you'll both be able to make purple.")

3. By allowing time for inner process. ("Lucy will let you know when she's ready to share.")

4. By showing appreciation for sharing when it occurs spontaneously. ("Thank you for giving me a bite of your cookie. It was delicious.")

5. By modeling sharing yourself. ("Now I want to give you a bite of my cookie.")

What should you do if you notice the older child deliberately taking advantage of the younger one? My son and daughter will be playing with baseball cards, and she'll keep the best ones for herself and give him the old beat-up ones. Should I say anything to her?

As long as both parties are satisfied, it's a good idea to refrain from interfering. It might help if you keep in mind that your son won't be a push-over forever. Very soon he'll be as big as, smart as, and confident as his older sister. He'll learn to speak up for himself and get what he needs. After all, he has an excellent teacher.

A lot of the fighting in my house starts when one of the boys "tells" on the other. Is there a way to discourage tattling?

It helps to know what motivates the "tattler." Is it simply a desire to get his brother in trouble? If that's the case, you wouldn't want to reward him with your anger at his sibling: "What? Your brother did that? You tell him to get in here this instant!" But suppose your son feels he really does need your help to protect himself from his brother's words or actions? Then what? How do you determine whether it's time for you to intervene?

One father reported that the tattling stopped in his home when he stopped judging and punishing. He said he told his kids that he expected them to really listen to each other and work out their differences on their own. But if they've made a good-faith effort and they're still stuck, he's always there to help. He was careful to add, "If any one of you sees someone doing something that could be dangerous, then you're to report to Mom or me as fast as your legs can carry you. We all have to look out for each other's safety in this family."

Yesterday my kids followed me from room to room, screaming, "It's my turn!" . . . "No, it's my turn!" They seem to insist upon doing their fighting on top of me. Any suggestions?

You can be equally insistent on protecting yourself. You can tell them, "I can hear how important it is for you two to decide whose turn it is to use the swing, but I need quiet now. You can work out your solution in your bedroom or outside. Not here!"

Children have a right to argue, and you have a right to protect your eardrums and your nervous system.

How do you feel about telling the kids to settle their argument by tossing a coin?

The problem with that suggestion coming from a parent is its underlying message: Your feelings and thoughts aren't important. Let chance determine your fate.

Another problem with tossing a coin is that you get a winner and a loser—usually a sore loser.

The only time I was able to use a "coin-toss" successfully was after all options for a solution had been explored. Then, if there was still an impasse I'd ask, "How would you both feel about tossing a coin? Could you live with the decision either way?"

Last Sunday my boys were arguing over whether we should go to the park or the beach. Should I have suggested that we all put it to a vote?

Voting can create bad feelings, particularly when the vote becomes a substitute for hearing each child's point of view: "Okay, let's not waste time arguing. We'll take a vote. Park or beach? Four for beach, one for park. Beach wins. Let's go everybody." No wonder the child who is in the minority feels betrayed by this form of "democracy."

The times when I couldn't get a consensus through discussion and was driven to call a vote (it was either that or spend the day at home discussing how to spend the day), I made it a point to say aloud (after the cheers of the winners subsided) what I thought might be the feelings of the loser. "We're going to the beach, because that's what the majority voted for. But I want everyone here to know that one person is disappointed. Andy was really looking forward to going to the park today." That usually stopped the gloating and comforted the loser.

It upsets me when we try to have a nice day out with the three girls and the bickering never stops. Is there anything we can do about it?

Different children at different times in their lives are better off with less "togetherness" with their siblings. They can use separate outings, separate friends, separate interests, separate activities, separate hours to be alone with a parent. With enough time apart, they might even begin to look good to each other.

What gets me is when the children finally do something nice and then fight over who has done the best job or the most work. My daughter will say, "I did all the dishes." My son

says, "Big deal. I had to do the pots, and take out the gar-
bage." How do you handle that?

When children vie for recognition over who has been most
helpful, it's a marvelous opportunity for the parent to validate
their cooperative achievement: "Hey, look at this kitchen! Between
the two of you, you got it all straightened up. That's what I call
great teamwork!"

Suppose we use the skills we've talked about in this course
and one child continues to make life miserable for the others.
What then?

If a child's relationship with his brothers and sisters seems to
be dominated by hatred, intense jealousy, and constant competi-
tiveness; if he can never share; if he's always abusing his siblings
physically and/or verbally, then it would be wise to seek professional help for this youngster. The parent might want to consider
individual therapy for the child or family therapy.

The Stories

I was agitated as I drove to our final session. Now that the course
was coming to an end, I was filled with doubts. Had I covered it
all? Had I ever warned the group how dangerous it was to make
one child a "confidante" with whom you discuss the problems
of a brother or sister? Had I ever mentioned that when you're
spending time alone with one child, it isn't a good idea to talk

about another? Had I brought up the sad fact that certain children would never get along, no matter how skilled the parent? I had been meaning to point out that even in those cases, by using skills, at least you wouldn't be making matters worse . . . If only there were a little more time . . .

The mood in the room as I entered contrasted sharply with my own. People were chatting happily. It was like the last day of school before summer vacation. No more instruction. Just story time. The chance to sit back and listen to tales of sibling strife being handled by other parents. The lightheartedness of the group was contagious. I found myself relaxing.

I took my seat and we began. The stories seemed to arrange themselves naturally. As soon as one person told about putting a particular skill into action, others quickly added their matching experiences. For example, the first two accounts both show parents making a conscious decision, for the first time, *not* to settle their children's fights for them. In each case, oddly enough, the object of contention was a chair.

I was feeling generous and decided to give the kids a treat. They could eat their supper on snack tables in the den and watch TV.

They were thrilled and ran off to the den to await their sandwiches. The next thing I heard was shrieking. They were fighting over the same chair. After a while Jason gave up, because Lori, being older and bigger, physically took over the chair.

Jason came into the kitchen screaming and crying. He wanted me to go in and claim the chair for him. I was tempted to, because Lori always gets her way, but instead I said, "Jason, I can see how angry you are. I think you should tell Lori how you feel."

He went back into the den to confront her. It was like throwing him to the lions. I heard her become so abusive that I ran in and said, "No name-calling in this family!"

Then she started in on me: "He's a spoiled brat! He always gets this chair! I never get a chance!"

I said, "I hear how strongly you both feel about this." Then I turned off the TV and announced, "It's up to you and Jason to find a solution." She also got my other message: *No TV until a solution is reached.*

I walked back into the kitchen with a crying Jason following me. I was fuming inside. It was all Lori's fault. I could have clobbered her. But I decided to give it one more go, and without much faith, I said, (loud enough for Lori to hear) "I feel sure you two can reach a solution if you really try."

At this point (I could hardly believe it) Lori came in and said, "Jas, I have a good idea." Jason got very excited and ran into the den with her. Next thing I knew they were picking up their sandwiches in the kitchen, happy and best of buddies.

I don't know what they worked out and I don't care. I'm so glad I held out and didn't take sides!

• • •

I'M THE ONE who's coming to class, but my husband is the one who's making changes, just from reading my notes. Yesterday morning, as we sat down to breakfast,

Billy and Roy started arguing about who was going to sit in the chair near the window. As the fighting escalated, my husband shouted out, "Nobody is going to sit in this chair—except me!"

He then hauled both boys off the chair and sat there himself. Billy responded by screaming, "I hate you, Daddy." The whole breakfast was quickly becoming a disaster.

Then something must have clicked in my husband's head. He said, "Gee Billy, I see how upset you are. It really was very important for you to sit here this morning."

Billy responded with a full-force. *"Yeah!"* and his anger just left him. Then my husband said, "I bet you and Roy could work out something that's fair to both of you."

To our amazement they started working out a plan where Billy would sit in the chair for breakfast and Roy would sit in it for dinner. Before I knew it, the whole atmosphere had changed, and we were all able to enjoy our breakfast.

Not everyone's children came up with solutions. But that didn't seem to matter. The very act of searching for a mutually agreeable alternative usually eased the tension between the siblings.

My wife was at work, and I was in bed with a bad cold, trying to get a little rest. For a while the boys (four and six) played beautifully. Then all of a sudden a big fight started, and they both rushed in to tell me their side.

I felt too rotten to listen to them, so I suggested that they draw their problem on the blackboard in their room, and when they were finished doing that, they could also draw what they thought would be a good solution.

They went for the idea. They got the ruler and divided the blackboard in half. Then each boy began to draw a picture on his side.

When they were finished, they brought me my bathrobe, and took me out of bed into their room to explain their pictures. It was clear that they were no longer angry. Somewhere along the way they must have made up.

• • •

Unfortunately, my three teenage girls have to share the same room. The worst part is when any one of them has a friend over. Yesterday there was the usual screaming about who should leave the room, and they all came storming down the stairs to complain to me, each one hoping I'd take her side.

But this time I wasn't going to get sucked in. I told them I expected *them* to work something out that would be fair to each of them.

They went back upstairs and were down again in two minutes. They said they tried, but couldn't, and I'd *have* to settle it.

I stuck to my guns.

Me: What? You gave it only two minutes? On a problem this big? You've got a situation where three girls are sharing one room and all of them want privacy when a friend comes over. You'll need more than two minutes to figure out that one.

Them: Come on, Dad, just tell us what to do.

Me: Think about it some more.

Them: It takes too long!

Me: Too long? Do you know how long it took the wisest men from thirteen different states to come to an agreement so that they could write a constitution and finally form the United States of America? Not days. Not weeks. **Years!** Your problem will take a lot of time. A lot of thought. But there's not a doubt in my mind that you can work it out—sooner or later.

They couldn't fight history. They went back into their room, and I could hear them talking seriously for the next fifteen minutes.

Well I'm sorry to report that they never did arrive at any specific agreements. *But,* over the next two weeks I did notice a distinct change in their attitude toward each other. Now when one of them has a friend over, the others will either leave the room or ask if it's okay to stay. That may not seem like much, but with my three, it's a major achievement.

The next two stories were about kids who did manage to arrive at solutions. To everyone's surprise these very young children were able to come up with creative answers to problems that would have stumped many a grown-up.

I was driving in the car last week with my daughter (six), her friend, and my son (three). The two girls each had two acorns and my son had none. He began to cry because neither of the girls would share theirs.

My daughter explained that if she gave Joshua one of her acorns, she would have fewer acorns then her friend. I told them that if they gave it some thought, they'd be able to find a solution that was fair to all. (I said it, but I didn't believe it.)

About a minute later, my daughter said, "Mommy, I found a solution! Johanna (the friend) could give Joshua one of her acorns. Then I will give you one of mine. That way we will each have one!"

• • •

WHEN MY sister-in-law came to visit me with her children, I was anxious to show off my new skills. (She thinks courses on child rearing are only for insecure parents.) Anyway, my nephew Johnny, age five, came running in to complain that my daughter Leslie, six, wouldn't let him be Spiderman. I said, "Oh boy, Johnny, that's a tough problem. You both want to be Spiderman. Hmmm . . . Well, I have confidence that you and Leslie can come up with a solution that's acceptable to both of you."

Under her breath my sister-in-law muttered that Johnny would give in to Leslie, "the way he always does," and let her be Spiderman.

In less than five minutes both children ran in excitedly. They had found a solution! *Both of them* would be Spiderman! And Leslie's younger brother, nineteen months, and Johnny's sister, three years, could be whatever they wanted to be.

My sister-in-law was quite impressed. She couldn't believe that such young children could work things out without their parents telling them what to do.

This next example came from a mother of teenagers. As you'll see her attitude is "better late than never."

I wish I had known all this stuff ten years ago. It's a lot easier to do it right when your kids are young than to start undoing when they're in their teens. But I figure I've still got a few years left to try to civilize them.

Dinner time is the worst. They do nothing but pick-pick-pick at each other while I'm trying to eat. I've told them a hundred times how disgusting they are, and that they sound like horse's patooties, but it never seems to register.

Anyway after last week's discussion, I decided to change my tactics. I wouldn't let anything get by me. The minute I heard the first put-down, I stopped them. I said, "Hey, no toxic talk!" Or, "That's a killer statement." Or, "You have a choice, kids—pleasant conversation or *no conversation!*"

I also told them that tomorrow I wanted them to come to dinner prepared with an interesting topic for discussion. I made it clear that I expected each of them to make a "contribution" to the good mood of our family.

You have no idea how determined I was. The next night I came to the table with my old whistle around my neck. (I used to be a gym teacher.) They got off to a good start. They were actually talking like normal people. But about five minutes into the discussion, I heard the first snide remark, and I blew my whistle. For a second they didn't know what I was up to, but then they caught on and laughed. And for the rest of the meal, they behaved decently.

Most of the accounts so far show siblings squabbles being resolved fairly quickly with little more than a brief intervention on the parent's part. Then there are the other kind, the kind that cause parents to shout, "Wait till you have children of your own. Then you'll know what aggravation is!" These last two accounts show parents involved in protracted mediation between angry siblings:

Wednesday afternoon.

Hal and Timmy arrive home from school. I greet them and ask about their day.

Hal says that he forgot his lunch, and that all his friends would give him were a couple of potato chips. I commiserate with him and give him the lunch he left behind. Then both boys go off to play.

In a few minutes they're back, shoving each other around, with Timmy in tears.

Me: What happened?

Hal: (Angrily) Timmy hit me on the head!

Timmy: (Tearfully) *By accident.* Hal, it was an accident!

Hal: No it wasn't! I know you did it on purpose. (He starts to shove Timmy again.)

Me: (Separating them) Okay, no matter what, people are not for hitting. Let's sit down and hear what's going on.

Hal: I don't want to talk about it.

Hal sits down and begins looking at a book Timmy brought home from the school library. Timmy takes it away from him. Hal grabs it back.

Hal: I'm looking at it.

Timmy: It's my book.

Hal: No it isn't. You got it from the library. That doesn't make it yours.

They are both pulling on the book.

Me: Now we have another problem. Two kids and one book. How are you going to solve it?

Timmy: I don't want him to read the book because he hit me.

Hal: Only because you hit me. I want revenge!

Timmy: It was an accident! And I didn't even hit you hard.

Hal: Oh yeah? You hit me hard, like this. (Hits Timmy on head.)

Timmy dodges, picks up a piece of cardboard and taps Hal gently with it: "No, it was lightly, like this."

Hal grabs the cardboard and hits Timmy in earnest.

Me: (Separating them) This looks like real fighting.

Hal: You're darn right it is!

Me: Hal, I can feel your anger. It is not safe for you to be around Timmy right now. I want you to go upstairs.

Hal: I'm not going. I want revenge!

Me: Hitting is not allowed! You can either go upstairs until you cool off, or you can talk to me about the things that are upsetting you.

Hal reluctantly goes up about three steps and then comes down again.

Hal: Mommy, he hit me so hard it gave me a headache.

Me: Ohhhh. And now you have a headache.

Hal: And it's not the first headache I've had today!

Me: You had a headache in school?

Hal: Yeah, in music, Miss Cane had a fit and did nothing but scream at me.

Me: (Suddenly getting the picture) Let me see, Hal. You've had a rough day. First you get to school and find that you forgot your lunch, then your music teacher yells at you . . .

Hal: (Who has been nodding agreement) And then at recess, Louis and Steven ganged up on me, and Bobby would have joined them if the playground aides hadn't stopped them . . .

He goes on to recount everything that had upset him at school. When it's all detailed, I acknowledge what a difficult day it must have been for him. That takes care of it. He and his brother play peacefully for the rest of the afternoon.

• • •

MY SON and stepson are close in age, and it's been a big adjustment for them to share a room after being used to having their own. One of the worst problems is that each of them insists upon listening to "his" music at the same time. Yesterday there were two radios in the same bedroom going full blast. One playing jazz, the other rock.

Me: (at the door) THE SOUND! THE SOUND! (Both radios are turned down.)

A day later it starts again—one rock station and one jazz station. I fly in a note folded like an airplane, "STOP THE MUSIC!"
It quiets down for a while.
Then I hear that noise again.

Me: ONE KIND OF MUSIC AT A TIME!

That's a great rule. It starts a fight. Each wants his own—right then—and accuses the other of having dumb taste.

Bedtime. Another fight. Todd wants to go to sleep to Chick Corea. Jeremy wants the Beatles. Can't have both; we have none. Todd comes to tell me how much better things were before Jeremy came. That night my husband tells me Jeremy has the same complaint about Todd.

Next day: The music is blaring again. I go in and calmly unplug both radios, put them on my dresser, and close the door to my room. When I hear the banging on the door and the cries of "No fair!," I open the door and announce, "As soon as you two can come up with a plan where the whole family's needs are met, you'll have them back."

A whole day of peace. I can think again. Part of the problem is space. If each kid had a little space of his own . . . But where? There's an alcove in the basement that's paneled and has an outlet, but you can't even get in there. It's filled with furniture and cartons from two households. The other part of the problem—probably the biggest part—is the growing resentment between the boys. Somehow we've got to get that out into the open.

I go through my class notes, consult with my husband, and we both decide to call our first family meeting. The boys are suspicious, but willing to go along.

We explain the ground rules and ask each of them to tell us some of the things that are bothering them. They're a little slow getting started, but once they do, it's hard to stop them:

"I hate having to share a room. I'm used to having my own."

"I feel like a stranger invading privacy."

"I don't get enough privacy. Sometimes I feel sorry for myself."

"We're too different. He's preppie. I'm . . . like punk."

"I can't get used to 'food rationing.' There are so many food rules around here. I used to be able to eat whatever I wanted."

"I don't like sharing my Dad. Why do we always have to do everything together?"

It's more than we bargained for. I have no idea of where to go from here and signal to my husband for help. He gives me his "I'm-out-of-my-depth" look. Then he says, "Your mother and I take your complaints seriously, and we want to think more about what you've told us. Let's continue our discussion tomorrow morning." Then I go off to do some errands, and my husband sits down to pay bills.

When I come home a few hours later, I hear noises in the basement and go down to investigate. Todd sees me and shouts, "Hey Mom, you're just in time. Come see what we did!"

Jeremy calls out, "Dad, you come too!"

We can't believe our eyes.

The basement is spotless. The cartons are piled against one long wall in neat stacks of three. The alcove has a scatter rug on the floor, a chair in the center, a lamp in one corner, a guitar in the other corner and a table against the wall with a radio on it.

My husband is speechless. I'm so amazed all I can get out is, "Oh! You did this?! Oh my . . ."

Jeremy: This is my music place.

Todd: That's because Jeremy likes to sit and play the guitar when he listens to rock. I get the bedroom because I like to lie on my bed to listen to my music.

Todd retreats to his bed and turns on a CD. Jeremy picks up his guitar and turns on the radio, and we go back to the living room and smile at each other like two happy fools. We both know it can't last, but for the moment, ah peace, it's wonderful!

This final story brought our last session to an end. From the expression on people's faces I could see they were already feeling nostalgic. I was too. We had shared many warm and memorable moments together.

"I'm going to miss these meetings," someone said.

"Do we *have* to end? I can use this course until the kids grow up and leave home."

"Could we meet again, about a month from now—just to have a refresher?"

I looked at the group questioningly. Several people nodded eagerly. Others were uncertain, mentioning summer plans and previous commitments.

I hadn't considered having another meeting. Yet the thought of a follow-up session one month from now, even with part of the group, was tempting.

We took out our calendars and set a date.

SEVEN

Making Peace
with the Past

I knew we weren't going to have a full house. Once the rhythm of the regular meeting schedule is broken, all kinds of obligations come crowding in, pushing aside one's best intentions. Nevertheless, I was so accustomed to the bristling energy and high spirits of a large group that it took me a moment to adjust to the fact that there would only be six of us this evening.

"Never mind," I thought to myself. "Six can be good too. Relaxed and intimate." But something else was going on here tonight. There was an undercurrent of tension in the room. I motioned to the group to draw their chairs into a tighter circle.

"So," I began, "how's it going?"

A long uneasy silence.

Finally . . . "I had quite a talk with my sister, Dorothy, a few weeks ago, but I guess I shouldn't take up anyone's time with that."

"It's your time," I said. "We have no prepared agenda tonight."

"But we're supposed to be talking about our children's sibling relationships, not ours."

"This session is for any sibling-related matter that's on your mind."

She hesitated. "Actually," she said, "I suppose it is relevant, because I never would have spoken to her if it hadn't been for these meetings."

There was sudden intense interest. Several people urged her on.

"Well, I don't know if any of you remember my mentioning my sister here before . . ."

"I remember very well," a woman said. "We were talking about comparing children and you told us how your mother always held Dorothy up to you as a model and how devastating that was for you."

The color rose in her face. "That's right," she said. "When I left that meeting, I was upset all over again . . . with my mother for putting Dorothy so far above me, and with Dorothy for always acting so superior.

"Then a few weeks later when we talked about casting children in roles and how hurtful that could be, even to the child who's been cast in a positive role, it dawned on me that maybe Dorothy had suffered too. For the rest of the night I couldn't get that thought out of my head, and when I woke up the next morning I knew I had to talk to her."

She paused and looked at us questioningly. "Are you sure you want to hear all this? There's so much more to tell."

Again the group urged her on.

"I felt a little anxious about calling, because outside of holidays, Dorothy and I have no contact with each other, so I didn't know how I'd be received. I suppose I was afraid I'd end up feeling 'wrong' again. Well it wasn't that way at all. Dorothy seemed very glad to hear from me. We talked about our husbands and children for a while, and then I finally got around to mentioning the group and how much I was getting from it. She seemed interested, so I told her a little bit about our session on roles, and then I asked her if she thought that Mom had put us in roles.

"At first she said she didn't think so, but after a while, as she talked more about her childhood, she finally admitted that she did feel under pressure always being the one who was held up as the example.

"Then she said the most amazing thing. That there were times she even thought Mom was trying to keep us apart, and that she used to worry that if she ever became close to me, Mom would think less of her. Because she was supposed to be the special one, and I was the one Mom was always criticizing."

It took us all a few seconds to digest what she had said. "That must have been a shocking thing for you to hear," someone murmured.

"In a way. But on another level, I think I always knew it. The strange thing is, I didn't feel upset. I just felt bad for Dorothy. I told her that that must have been terrible for her, an awful burden for a child to bear. Then all of a sudden she started to cry.

"It was the first time I had ever experienced my sister as vulnerable. I wanted so much to comfort her, but she was a thousand miles away. I said, 'Dorothy, I'm hugging you. I'm reaching right through the phone and hugging you.'

"Then she told me how sorry she was for the pain she must

have caused me, and how much it meant to her that I had called, and that if I hadn't, we might have gone to our graves without ever knowing each other. Then I started to cry."

Several of us reached for our tissues.

"Do you know what Dorothy and I have decided to do?" she continued. "We're going to meet halfway between New York and Chicago in a hotel. We're going to spend a whole weekend together—just the two of us—no husbands, no kids, just us. We've got a lot of catching up to do."

"I'm happy for you," a man said, "but in a way it makes me sad too."

"Why?" Dorothy's sister asked.

"Well it's sad to think that parents would divide their own children like that. I know how hard it was on our family when my father kept my older brother, Tom, away from the rest of us."

"Why would he do that?" she asked.

"Well, it's a long story . . . the main thing is that Tom was always a rebel, and my father came from this strict, Greek Orthodox tradition and there were always terrible fights between them. The final break came when Tom was seventeen. He took cash from my father's store and ran off with it. My father never forgave him—never. And he never let Tom back in the house. My mother pleaded with him. I pleaded with him. He wouldn't budge."

"And you never saw Tom again?"

"Once. Eight years later, when my father died, Tom came to the funeral with his wife, but since then we've had very little contact. I'm all for inviting him for Thanksgiving, Christmas, other family occasions, but Nick, my younger brother, always objects. He refuses to have anything to do with him."

"That's strange," she said. "It's almost as if he's taken over for your father."

"I know. Nick has put me in a very difficult position. Right now I'm torn. You see my youngest son is going to be christened next month and I want Tom to be there. I know what he did was wrong, but it could have been handled differently. He shouldn't have been excommunicated from the family. Because what have we got now? My children have an uncle and aunt they don't know, cousins they never see. And I have a niece and nephew who are strangers to me."

"What are you going to do?" Dorothy's sister asked softly.

Long pause. "I'm going to talk to Nick again. We've been blessed with a brother and we *must* take him in and show him love. Anything else would be wrong. I want all of my brothers together, to be with me at my son's christening. I want us to be a whole family again."

"Oh how I wish it for you," another woman said wistfully. "It must be wonderful to have even the possibility of being a whole family again."

I wondered at her comment. Then I remembered that this was the woman who, at our first meeting, had mentioned having an emotionally disturbed sister.

"There'd be no point in trying to reconnect with my sister," she went on. "The last time I tried to speak to her, she accused me of spreading rumors about her to her friends.

"Besides, the person I really wanted to talk to was my mother. Being in this course has opened up my eyes about a lot of things. After we had our final session, I said to myself, 'If it's the last thing I do, I have to let my mother know how I've been feeling all these years.'"

"Do you think you ever will?" someone asked tentatively.

"I already did," she answered.

"And your mother actually listened?"

"Well, it wasn't easy for her."

"What did you tell her?"

She hesitated and looked at me uncomfortably.

"You may not want to talk about it," I offered.

"Oh, I don't know . . . ," she said. "I guess I don't mind." She closed her eyes for a moment, trying to reconstruct the scene. "Basically, what I told my mother was how much I resented it that Lynn's emotions had always ruled the house. I said, 'You were so obsessed with Lynn and her problems that you never saw me. You never knew who I was and never cared to know. So I never really felt loved.'"

You could have heard a pin drop. "What did she say to that?" someone asked.

"She said I was being ridiculous, particularly since I was the perfect child, the one everyone *did* love.

"I said, 'You see—that's just what I'm talking about. You're doing it again! Making me into something that's not even real.'

"My mother ignored me and launched into the same old story again about what a strain it had been for her to have to deal with a disturbed child all these years—all the running to doctors, the crazy behavior, never a moment's peace. She went over all the times Lynn did this and Lynn did that . . .

"I had heard it too often. I couldn't let her finish. I said, 'Mother, I'm going to ask you to do something that's going to be very difficult. *Listen to me. Just listen* and don't try to explain anymore. I know all those things already. I want you to try to understand what it's been like for *me* all these years.'

"She stared at me. Then she said, 'All right . . . all right, go ahead.'

"Well it just poured from me. I reminded her of all the times she tried to make me into some kind of paragon.

" 'Thank goodness, *you're* trustworthy.'

" 'At least *you've* got your head on straight.'

" 'I'm glad I have one child who is responsible.'

"And I dragged up everytime I tried to rebel, like when I cut school once in the fifth grade, or when I refused to play the piano for company, and how all I ever heard was, 'That's not like you, dear.' I couldn't give enough examples of how invisible I felt. No wonder I didn't know who I was half the time.

"Then I asked her, 'Do you know what it would have meant to me if just once you had said, "You don't have to be so good all the time. You don't have to be so perfect. You don't have to be mother's pleasure. You can be nasty, bratty, sloppy, mean, inconsiderate, irresponsible—and it's okay. It's normal to be those ways at times. And I'll love you just as much."'

"Tears were streaming down my mother's face as I was talking, but I didn't stop. I couldn't. Finally, when I was through, she whispered, 'I had no idea . . . What can I say? . . . I don't know what to say.'

"I said, 'Nothing. There's nothing to say. I just wanted you to know.'

"Then something dissolved inside of me. I said, 'Don't think I don't know what you've been through with Lynn all these years. Don't think I don't know how hard it's been for you.' Then I put my arms around her, and we held each other and I felt as if a wall had come down between us."

I listened in wonder. How swiftly understanding frees us to

forgive. What an enormous relief it must have been to let go of all those bitter feelings. And what a great gift her mother gave her, just by listening.

"I could never tell my mother anything like that," another woman said, shaking her head. "She could never deal with my feelings. She can't even deal with her own feelings. I don't know why I bothered, but recently I tried to tell her some of the things that had hurt me when I was a child, like how I wasn't ever allowed to get mad at my brother, and how I always had to kow-tow to him because he was the crown prince.

"You know what she said? 'The trouble with you is you notice problems and you want everything to be perfect.'

"Then I said, 'What's the matter with saying you're hurt when you're hurt? If you bump into the bed, and stub your toe, can't you say, "Gee, that hurt like hell!" '

"She said, 'Nah, I just walk away and say, "Wasn't that stupid!" Then I just forget about it.' And that's how my mother deals with everything. So how could I expect her to understand me?

"She's so dense, sometimes I feel like shaking her. All she ever talks about is how she wants her children to be close, but everything she's ever done has driven us further apart. . . . You know what's really weird? My brother—who never calls me—has just had his first baby, and suddenly he's been calling me for advice. We've actually been talking to each other like regular people. Maybe there's hope for us after all. But I swear, if we ever do get to be friends one day, it will be in spite of my mother, not because of her. I know she means well, but you couldn't exactly accuse her of being sensitive."

"I don't know," another man interjected. He was the only one who hadn't spoken so far. "My mother and father were both very sensitive people, but I can assure you, even sensitive parents will allow insensitive things to go on."

All eyes turned toward him.

"I think I once mentioned," he explained, "that I had a twin brother who used to beat me up, and they didn't make a move to stop him."

"That's terrible," someone said. "Why not?"

"I have no idea. Maybe they thought that boys should have a certain amount of rough and tumble. Maybe they thought that because we were twins, we had this natural affinity and wouldn't ever really hurt each other.

"I don't know what they thought. All I can tell you is that when you're five years old, and the only protection you have are those parents, and if they're looking the other way, it can be pretty frightening. You figure somehow you just have to get through it."

"You must have been a tough kid to survive that," I said.

"I was tough. But Eric was a lot tougher. And a lot bigger. He was born five minutes ahead of me and was practically twice my birth weight."

"So from the very beginning, you were at a disadvantage."

"That's true. But in the early years I didn't care that he was so much bigger. I fought him anyway. Typical example: He'd come in and turn off my TV program because he decided he wanted to watch his. Well, I wasn't going to let him push me around. So I'd turn it back on again. Then he'd jump on me and hold me down and punch me until finally it was drilled into me that he could really hurt me. Then there was one point—it took a while—where he would come in and turn off the set, and I would just walk away."

"I still don't see how your parents could have allowed this to go on!" a woman exclaimed.

"Well, actually my mother did try to protect me, some of the time. She'd yell at Eric and take me in the room with her. But mostly she felt we should work it out ourselves. Once she bought us this Joe Palooka thing, a big plastic blow-up man with sand on the bottom that bounced back when you hit him, and I remember her saying to Eric, 'When you want to hit your brother, hit this instead.'

"I'll never forget it, because after we got this thing, he would hit me, then the bag, and then me. Obviously it didn't work."

"What about when you got to be teenagers?" someone asked.

"Eric became a super jock—hockey, soccer, football. He would fight to kill, to annihilate, to destroy. The worse you were beaten, the happier he was. I avoided sports. Actually I didn't venture much in high school. I tried to succeed socially. I never did anything that would take me out of my protective circle of friends."

"Didn't anything change between you as you got older?"

"Not really. The attacks just switched from physical to verbal. Like a big thing in our family were discussions at the dinner table. Eric was always up on everything—books, sports, politics. If I tried to contribute anything, he'd sneer, 'That's stupid.' And my father and mother were so busy being impressed by how knowledgeable he was, they never even noticed. So after a while, I just listened in on their discussions and made humorous cracks. Actually I developed a rather sharp, sarcastic tongue. It was my only weapon against Eric. And I used it. I knew all his weak spots."

"Who could blame you?" a man said, "You needed some way to get back at the bastard."

He raised his eyebrows and sat back in his chair—his whole demeanor changed. "At one time I would have agreed with you.

But the craziest thing happened. Last month when all these sessions were over, I had this strong desire to contact Eric again,
after years of avoiding him. So I called him, and we met for what
turned out to be a three hour lunch."

Curiosity ran high. "What did you talk about?" . . . "Did you
confront him?" . . . "Did you tell him how he loused up your life?"

"Mainly he wanted to tell me how I loused up *his* life."

Jaws dropped.

"According to Eric, I was the favorite son and he could never
forgive me for that. He pointed out that Mom and I had a natural
rapport with each other, and that the chemistry between him and
Mom was all wrong. He felt that she was always angry at him, and
busy protecting me, and that he never got the understanding he
deserved.

"He also told me that he remembered how right from the
beginning people were always attracted to me. He said, 'You were
so tiny, with these perfect features—like the littlest kitten in the
litter, and I was this big goofy looking kid. Everybody walked past
me and picked you up.'

"Then he told me how isolated and shy and awkward he felt,
even way back in Kindergarten, and how it was even worse in high
school because I was "Mr. Personality" and would come home
with lots of friends, and he would have nobody.

"I reminded him that he was the one who got all the praise in
the house for being such an intellect and such an athlete. He said,
'The praise didn't mean anything. You had the love.'

"I asked him, point blank, 'Is that why you beat me up?'

"He said, 'Damned right. I was mad and frustrated, and you
were my scapegoat.'

"Then I asked him if he thought that if Mom wasn't always so angry at him for beating me up, whether he would have been less angry with me.

"He said, 'Probably.' Then he asked me, 'Would you have been jealous if Mom and I got along real well?'

"I said, 'Maybe. But it sure would have been worth it, because then you wouldn't have been so mad at me.'

"Then it hit us how much we had both suffered, how we tore each other down, how the net result of him attacking me and my getting back in my own way was so hurtful to both of us.

"By the time we left each other, we each had a sense of completion, as if we had found a missing part of ourselves. And we knew we were both okay. It wasn't as if either one of us was an evil person. He was a nice guy, and I was a nice guy. Just two nice guys trying to grapple with the frustrations of being brothers. And two nice parents who had tried to do their best."

• • •

Our time was up. We were all spent. It had been an emotionally draining session. None of us had any more talk left in us. The goodbye hugs were hard and silent.

For the first time I was glad for the long drive home, and grateful for the silence in the car. There was a lot to think about.

I was awed by what I had just heard, awed at the power of the sibling dynamic to cause such pain between brothers and sisters, from earliest childhood on; awed at the almost magnetic pull between siblings to reconnect, to reestablish their "siblingship"; awed at the drive that pushes siblings, however wounded, back together to try to heal themselves and each other.

And I felt a resurgence of conviction about the skills I had been teaching. Every painful incident that was aired at tonight's session might have been lessened or avoided altogether if the adults in charge had had some skills.

"Imagine," I thought, "a world in which brothers and sisters grow up in homes where hurting isn't allowed; where children are taught to express their anger at each other sanely and safely; where each child is valued as an individual, not in relation to the others; where cooperation, rather than competition is the norm; where no one is trapped in a role; where children have daily experience and guidance in resolving their differences.

"And what if these children grow up to become the world shapers of tomorrow? What a tomorrow that would be! The kids brought up in such homes would know how to attack the world's problems without attacking our precious world. They would have the skills and the commitment to do it. They would save our global family."

It started to rain. I put on my windshield wipers and turned on the news.

Uncanny. It was like hearing the stories in our group, but only on a larger scale: disputes over territory, disputes over belief systems; the "have-nots" jealous of the "haves"; the big guys muscling in on the little guys; the little guys bringing their complaints to the UN and the World Court; long, complicated histories of bitterness and distrust being played out with invective and bombs.

But tonight it didn't get to me. Tonight I was overflowing with optimism. If after such long histories of pain and competition and injustice, the urge to reconcile still wells up so powerfully between siblings, then why not envision another kind of world? A world in which brothers and sisters of all nations, determined to resolve the grievances that separate them, reach out to each other, and discover for themselves the love and strength that one sibling can give to the other.

I turned off the radio. The rain was letting up.

Suddenly all things seemed possible.

Afterword

Dear Reader,

When Siblings Without Rivalry *climbed to the top of the* New York Times *best-seller list less than a month after publication, we were suddenly catapulted into the position of "sibling experts." Everyone wanted to talk to us. It seemed the subject we had written about was so central to so many people's lives that they felt compelled to tell us how it was for them with their siblings. Brothers and sisters, young and old, called us during radio interviews, challenged us on television shows, took us aside after lectures, poured out their hearts during workshops, and wrote us long, poignant letters. Even reporters from newspapers and magazines interlaced their interviews with tales of their own sibling angst.*

We listened and learned. Clearly there was more to know and more to say. And so when our editor asked if we would consider adding new material to our book for an updated edition, we didn't hesitate for a moment. Here was our golden opportunity.

We could give more help to parents of young children. More help to working parents whose older children were spending long, unsupervised hours together. More help to all parents who were looking for new ways to encourage good feelings and respectful behavior between siblings.

It is our hope that this afterword to Siblings Without Rivalry *will bring a new measure of harmony to your home.*

ADELE FABER AND ELAINE MAZLISH

Early Feedback

It was during the radio call-in shows on our publicity tour for *Siblings Without Rivalry* that we, once again, experienced the full fresh impact of how brothers and sisters mark each other's lives. Something about the anonymity of radio, about being able to talk unseen on the telephone, freed people to reveal their most personal feelings. Here's a sampling of what we heard:

> "I decided not to have a second child because I knew how much my older sister went through because of me. People in and out of the family were always commenting on how pretty and talented I was and ignoring her. I would never want any child of mine to suffer the way my sister did—and still does."

> "I could never be close with my brother. Maybe because of how we grew up. My father was a football coach and from day one he turned everything in the family into a competition. You had to beat out the other guy. My brother bought into it completely. Even today when I call him, he'll never say, 'Hi Joe, how're you doing?' or 'How're you feeling?' First thing out of his mouth is, 'Got a new car today' or something like that. He's still got to 'one up' me."

> "I'm one of three sisters—all close in age—and I still remember asking my mother, over and over again, 'Who do you love best?' Her answer never changed. She'd always

say, 'I love you all the same. You're like my three little bears.' Well, let me tell you, that hurt. It really hurt. In my mother's eyes I was nobody special. It isn't easy to go out and face the world thinking you're just one of three little bears."

"My father wanted each of his children to feel special, so he'd tell me, 'You're smart,' and then tell my brother, who was no great student, 'but you're good with people.' I took his words as gospel. I'd either hang back in social situations or avoid them all together. Only recently—and I'm in my thirties—did it begin to dawn on me that maybe my father was wrong. After all, there are a lot of people who seem to like me.

Anyway, after reading your book, I began thinking about how it was for my brother and how my father's words must have affected him, too, and whether that was why he dropped out of school and why he always seemed resentful of me. Then I really got upset.

I thought, why did my father feel he had to ration out our abilities as if they were somehow mutually exclusive? Why couldn't he have said that there was room for more than one smart person in the family? Why couldn't he have boasted that *both* of his kids were bright and *both* of his kids were good with people. That would have meant everything to us."

"My parents did the opposite of everything you recommend in your book. Recently I told my sister (she's forty-one and still mad at me for being the 'good one'), 'Look, let's not let all the dumb things Mom and Dad did to us when we were kids spoil our relationship forever. I love you. I think you're a beautiful person. I really do. And I need you and want you in my life.' "

Even children called in to tell us how unhappy they were about their sibling relationships.

A girl complained about her brother who "always starts up with me, but I'm the one who gets punished." Another girl spoke of a "mean" older sister who was supposed to be baby-sitting for her but who pushed her out of the house and wouldn't let her back in until just before her parents got home.

A ten-year-old boy told us; "Me and my brother are always having arguments with each other. We fight so much that if you locked us both in a car overnight and opened the door in the morning, we'd both be dead. Is your book just for grown-ups or can kids read it too?"

• • •

WHEN WE RETURNED from our publicity tour, we found our mailbox stuffed with letters from people who wanted to share their reactions to our new book. Here are excerpts from some of those letters and others that followed in the years to come.

I stayed up until the wee hours of the morning reading *Siblings Without Rivalry*. At 6:30 A.M. I awoke and used my newfound skills to get my two daughters up and ready for school. What a difference a day makes! Yesterday my nine-year-old skipped breakfast because she didn't want to sit at the table and look at her sister's 'ugly face.' I nearly had to carry her onto the school bus. My three-year-old whined and shrieked her way through her morning routine as she and her sister fought, bickered, and tattled.

This morning, though, when the first tattle came from the older one ("Mom, dance class isn't 'til this afternoon, but Sally is wearing her tap shoes already."), I said, 'Well, I'm not interested in what Sally's doing right now. But I'd love to talk about you.' My nine-year-old was nonplussed. I used a few more of my newfound skills, and before I knew what had happened, both my daughters had a leisurely breakfast, took turns sweetly allowing me to fix their hair, and actually waved good-bye to each other.

I'm still puzzling over this, though: On the trip to preschool my three-year-old said, 'Mom, I don't want to be nice anymore today. Can I be mad now?'"

Some people didn't wait to finish the book. This letter came from a mother of three who had just completed the first chapter:

Last week was the worst week of my life. My oldest, Ashley (6), said she hated her sister, Loren (4). "I hate her," she said, "but I like Melissa (the baby). She doesn't take my things."

I was destroyed. My children hated each other. How could I deal with this? I was so distraught I went downstairs to the bookshelf and picked up my unread copy of *Siblings Without Rivalry* and started to read it. This was on Friday—the end of my horrible week. By Saturday morning I had just about digested chapter one when Ashley came down the steps crying, "Loren broke my chalk! Now I can't use it!"

Me: Oh.

Ashley: She broke *three* pieces! She always gets into my things. She breaks everything.

Me: Oh, Ashley, I can see how very upset and angry you are. [I stopped here because that was all I had read and I didn't know what to do next.]

Ashley: I have an idea! Remember the old chalkboard in the toy closet? Why don't we give it to Loren and get her her own chalk.

Me: (Amazed) I like that idea! Let's do it.

Thanks Adele and Elaine. I have more confidence now and can't wait to read the rest of the book.

As we were congratulating ourselves at the power and clarity of the work we had created, along came this letter:

Dear Ms. Faber and Ms. Mazlish,

I would like to know if you can send me *any* information available on sibling rivalry. I have just read *Siblings Without Rivalry*. I have two daughters, ages ten and seven, that are driving me *nuts!* No matter what I try, they still fight like cats and dogs. One day I was so frustrated I told them to go outside and search through all the trashcans for their dinner since they are fighting like alley cats and dogs. I couldn't believe I said that! Please help.

That took us down a peg. We had this fantasy that we could solve everyone's sibling problems. This next letter lifted our spirits.

I just want to let you know how wonderful your book is. I grew up in the most dysfunctional family. I sneer at books that seem to have *all* the answers. I always find that I cannot sensibly apply them to my own life. Your book, however, was incredibly useful in my life and my situation. Thank you for caring enough to write it.

Some parents wrote to tell us how our book inspired them to come up with ideas of their own. A father wrote:

With my three boys it's always "I want to be first" and tears from those who aren't. It goes on about everything—who's first to get into the car, who's first to get a cookie, a kiss goodnight—whatever.

Recently I created what I think is a great reply. I said, "You are *first* to be second." It worked! The second one proudly said, "Ha! I'm second, *first*." But the big thing I want them to realize is that each one of them is first with me.

The mother of a six- and eight-year-old wrote:

The skills in your book work like a charm with my two girls—*except* when they both want the same thing at the same time. Then they each get a "death grip" on whatever the thing happens to be, and no matter what I say or how I say it, they won't let go. They're so busy with their tug-of-war they don't even hear me.

Now here's my big discovery: The only way to break the deadlock is to take the object away from them. The trick is not to do it punitively "Okay, that's it! Now neither one of you gets it," but rather by pointing them to the task that needs to be done. I say, "I'll just put this on the shelf here for safekeeping while you two work out a plan for how to share it without fighting. As soon as you're ready, let me know and I'll take it down."

The first time I did that, they both started by trying to appeal to me. "Okay, Mom, I'll have it first and then Angie can have it in five minutes." I said, "You need to talk to Angie about that." I had to keep pointing them back to each other. By now, though, they get the idea and they're actually pretty good at negotiating directly with each other.

P.S. I still haven't figured out the next step—namely, how to put them in charge from the very beginning and keep me out of it altogether. I'm thinking of suggesting to them that just in case it happens again, *they* designate a neutral spot in the house where they can put a contested object until they both decide what to do about it.

I'll let you know what happens.

Because *Siblings Without Rivalry* was translated into over thirty languages, we also received many letters from abroad. This one came from France:

Like many people I thought I could avoid sibling rivalry, but from the first day of my pregnancy, Claude didn't want the baby. He kept asking me why I was having it and I gave the reply: "Daddy and I love you so much we wanted another baby." (He must have loved that!) Until one day I told him the truth. "I didn't mean to make this baby at all and sometimes I wish I never had!" He never asked me again.

Marie was born when Claude was just three years old. All during my pregnancy he'd say things like, "Put the baby in the rubbish bin." Then it was in the rubbish truck, where it would "get all mashed up." Other days he'd "put her in the gutter and the rain would wash her right to Australia" to his grandparents. I just listened to it all and nodded. Friends were pretty shocked about that, but I hoped the listening would do away with the jealousy. It didn't. As they both got older (he's six, she's three), Marie proved to be more and more charming, delightful, and outgoing. She's exactly the opposite of Claude, who is very shy and introverted and finds it difficult to make friends. Things got steadily worse. What I hated most was the way Claude would constantly annoy his sister for no reason whatsoever. It really gets to me.

I told Claude I love him as much as Marie but that didn't seem to satisfy him. I explained that a mother's love always keeps growing, but more and more, he measures what he gets compared to her—she has more time with me, more cuddles, more time with daddy than he does. I told him life is not "equal," but that didn't seem to solve anything.

Yesterday a friend gave me *Siblings Without Rivalry*. I finished it late in the afternoon so I've had an evening and morning to put it into practice. The results are wonderful! They've had only one fight so far this morning, which is a sheer miracle, and they managed to work out a satisfactory solution for both of them. I also wrote down all their grievances, as well as what they liked about each other. Very successful. After Marie said she liked it when Claude read to her, he sat right down and read her six books!

A few months later, we received a follow-up letter from the same mother:

My house is transformed! So often now I'll hear Marie cry and then Claude say, "No, no, don't cry, Marie. I didn't mean to. Let's find a solution." I don't hear any more comments about Marie having more cuddles, more clothes, more toys. A week after I drew up the list of what they did and didn't like about each other, we consulted the list again. Marie's first comment was, "I like Claude. He's nice to me." The effect on Claude was amazing. It was the most perfect reinforcement of his new and better behavior to her.

Here's another example: About a month ago, Marie said she was afraid to go to her cupboard (a little cubbyhole next to their bedroom) because "Claude says there's a wolf there." I was about to tell Claude how stupid it was to frighten his sister, but then I thought, "What would Adele and Elaine say?" Then I said, "Claude, can you go up to the cubbyhole and remove the wolf, please?"

Up he went. When he came back he told Marie he had killed the wolf and eaten it. That seemed to reassure her. Later Claude confessed to me that he told her about the wolf to stop her from changing her clothes all the time, which is one of her favorite activities, and one which drives me crazy too.

How can I ever thank you enough!

I. Coping with Young Rivals

Getting Off to a Good Start

One of the main topics that arose during the workshops we ran after our book was published was how best to handle the special problems that arise between siblings during their early years. Here are some observations and suggestions from the parents in our groups that we felt were especially valuable:

"It seems to me that the skills you talk about are much more likely to click in if there's an overall positive relationship between the kids. If they basically view each other as pests or nuisances or rivals, then there's not much motivation for them to respond to skills. If Dad says, 'That hug you just gave the baby made her cry,' big brother might secretly rejoice. So I think it's important from early on to do whatever you can to get those good feelings going between them. Kids need a lot of experience having good times together so that when the conflicts and fights come—as they must—they both have the memory of a positive relationship they want to get back to."

That statement led to nodding heads and many examples of how to accomplish the goal:

You Two Were Having So Much Fun

"When the kids are running wildly through the house and the big one accidentally crashes into the little one and the little one comes crying to me, 'Tony knocked me down,' I say, 'Oh no! You didn't want that to happen. You two were having so much fun together.' That seems to help both boys recoup much faster and remind them of their good relationship."

Listen to What the Boys Did Today!

"Sometimes I let my boys overhear me talking about the fun things they do when they're together. I'll tell my husband, in front of the kids, 'Do you know what Danny (four) taught Sam (two) today? He showed him how to jump from the stool to the beanbag chair.' Danny gives a big grin. 'And Sam had the idea of hiding under the beanbag chair and pretending to be a turtle.' And then Sam grins."

Ask Your Sister; She's Good at That

"Very often when my two-year-old asks me to help her with something, I deliberately direct her to her sister. I'll say, 'Ask Melissa to give you a hand with that. She's good at stringing beads or tying knots, or cutting things out'— or whatever. And before you know it the two of them are sitting on the floor working together."

Lucky Girl to Have Such a Brother

"The first time my three-year-old son walked in on me while I was cooing over the baby and telling her how precious she was, he looked devastated. So right away I switched to cooing about her brother. I went on and on in a singsong tone about what a lucky girl she was to have such a special brother who knew how to put on his own shoes and use the potty and ride a tricycle and anything else I could think of. David looked proud and happy and I felt very clever for figuring out a way to give each of them what they needed at the same time."

Fun Activities for All

"I try to think of as many activities as possible that my twenty-month-old and four-year-old can enjoy together. Tracy blows bubbles for Patty so Patty can pop them.

Tracy marches around the room while Patty bangs on the drum. One sits on a fire truck while the other one pushes. One drives the truck while the other is the traffic policeman who says when to stop and when to go. It all helps."

I Hear Crying

"Whenever I hear screaming or crying from the next room my first impulse is to run in and accuse the older one of hurting the younger one. I know how bad that would be for their relationship, yet I can't ignore the crying. Recently I came up with a great solution. I called out, 'I hear crying. Do you need help or can you work it out yourselves?' The first time I said it there was a long silence. Then I heard the big one say, 'We can work it out.' And that's what he says now most of the time when I use that approach. But he also feels free to call me in and tell me about the problem. And that's fine with me. I want both my boys to know that it's legitimate to ask for help when they need it."

You Two Are Some Team!

"I used to set up little contests between my four-year-old twin girls whenever I wanted them to do something fast. I'd say, 'Who can be the first to get dressed?' or 'Who can be the first to put away her toys?' Anything to get them moving. I'd get them moving all right, but the fallout was terrible. The winner would crow, 'Nyah, nyah, I beat you.' And the loser would cry and be mad at her sister.

"Then I read the suggestion in *Siblings Without Rivalry* about saying, 'You two are some team,' and I changed tactics. Now the contest is about the two of them beating the clock instead of each other. I'll say, 'I'm setting the timer for five minutes. Do you think you two can get your shoes and socks on before the buzzer goes off?' That little change made a big difference. Now they giggle and rush and help each other, and whether they beat the clock or not, I still say, 'You two are some team!' They light up when they hear that.

"And it makes me feel good too. Because I figure that if they learn to work as a team now, when they're so young, they'll know how to pull together when they're older."

Property Rights

A major source of frustration for parents of young children is the daily struggle over property rights. Parents who are doctors, lawyers, even heads of corporations are often stymied by the legal complexities of the "Mine! . . . No mine!" wars. "Yes, I know it's yours, but you haven't touched it in months, so why can't your sister play with it?" may sound perfectly reasonable to a parent's ears, but provoke earsplitting shrieks from the outraged owner. Then, when the judgment is reversed—"Oh, all right, give it to your brother. After all it *is* his"—more shrieking ensues from the newly deprived sibling. And consider the sheer number of toys to be adjudicated—the balls, the blocks, the dolls, the trucks. Who can even remember what Grandpa gave to which child last Christmas when both are loudly claiming ownership? These are not easy questions to resolve. Here are some of the thoughts and experiences of the parents in our group:

A Policy about Property

"I don't want to live in a family where we wrangle over every little thing. I think it's important to establish a general policy about property. I explain to my children (three and four-and-a-half) that most of the things in the house are for sharing. For instance, Daddy just bought himself a set of screwdrivers, but if I need to use one Dad won't say, 'No, you can't. It's mine.' And I just bought myself a new blender, but if Dad wants to use it, that's fine with me. I'd never say, 'Don't you dare touch it; it's mine.' So the general idea is that most things in the family can be used by anyone who happens to want or need them.

"But I also explained that some things are so special or so new or so delicate—like the camera Dad got for his birthday, or my new guitar—that they're not for sharing. Those things we keep in a special place and you have to ask permission if you want to use them. So, if there are any toys you don't want anyone else to touch or use, you can let each other know what they are and where you plan to keep them, and we'll respect that."

A Sign for Private Property

"In my house we assigned each girl her own shelf for her special things with her name and private property sign on it. That means if you want to use any of those toys, you *must* ask the owner first. But when the shelves start to bulge, as they do periodically, we review which toys absolutely have to remain there and which can be released to become community property."

A Strange Urge

"Theoretically, community property is a lovely idea. But I find as soon as my older boy sees his little brother playing with anything, he grabs it out of his hand. It's like he has some kind of compulsion. I used to yell at him, 'Stop that! What is wrong with you! Can't you see he was playing with it?' or, 'Leave your brother alone. He had it first!' But that didn't get me anywhere. Finally, I sat down with my big boy and we talked about what a strange thing it was—this urge to snatch something out of someone else's hand. 'Even though you know you're not supposed to, something inside you just wants to. There could be a hundred toys in the room, but somehow the best toy is the toy in someone else's hands.'

We talked about this a lot, as being a funny quirk that people have—not right or wrong, just something people feel. That conversation was a turning point. Many times now he'll start to grab from his brother and I'll stop him.

But he doesn't fight me anymore. We just look at each other and we both say out loud, sort of half sad, half smiling, 'The best toy is the toy in someone else's hands.'"

Grabbing: A Two-Step Strategy

"What helps me deal with the grabbing is the idea of accepting the feelings but redirecting the unacceptable behavior. For instance if one of my girls snatches a toy from another, I'll say, 'Oh, Casey, you really want to play with Emily's bubble wand—right now. It's hard to wait. The rule is no grabbing things from anyone. But you can tell Emily you want to use it next. She's good at sharing.'

"Then I'll say to Emily, 'When you're finished blowing bubbles with your magic wand, would you please tell Casey because she wants to play with it next.' Then I take Casey's hand and say, 'Let's find another toy that's interesting while we're waiting.' The trick, and I can't always do it, is to try to take care of both of their needs and both of their feelings at the same time."

To Punish . . . or Not to Punish

One question kept coming up during many of our workshops: If one sibling—for whatever reason—hurts another, shouldn't he be punished? Especially if you told him a hundred times to "use words, not fists." Suppose he keeps on hitting? At one point, don't you have to take stronger measures? Shouldn't you deprive him of something he cares about, like his favorite TV show? or at least send him to "time out?"

We turned the question back to the group. The general consensus was that while punishment might stop the aggressor temporarily, the long-term effect would be to worsen the relationship. The aggressor now has reason to be even more resentful of his sibling, whom he sees as the cause of his punishment. And the victim is now less safe when left alone with his brother.

The same dynamics apply to "time out." One mother told of visiting her sister who had three-year-old twin boys. One of the boys took her by the hand, pointed to a chair in the corner of his room and said, "This is the thinking chair. I hit my brother. They put me in the thinking chair. I think about it. I get out. I hit him again."

But despite general agreement about the negative side effects of punishment and "time out," some doubts remained. One woman said, "I still think there are times when you have to punish. Just this morning Amy (she's four) pushed Billy so hard (he's only eighteen months old) that he fell over and banged the back of his head on the hard floor. He screamed hysterically and I went crazy. This isn't the first time she's done something like that to him. I told her she was a very bad girl and she should go to her "time out" corner and stay there until she learned how to behave. And that's where I left her when the baby-sitter came this morning. What else could I have done?"

Her challenge launched the group into a lively discussion. We all agreed that you couldn't allow the older child to go on hurting the younger one. On the other hand, some sympathy was expressed for the older child. It wasn't easy for any kid to have to put up with an eighteen-month-old brother or sister. Several parents described how their toddlers pulled toys away from older siblings, bit them, scratched them, and hit or screamed when they didn't get their way. We knew these toddlers were going through a normal developmental phase. Preverbal kids express their needs physically. Nevertheless, many in the group felt it was up to the parents to respond helpfully by teaching the older children how to handle the little ones in non-hurtful ways.

Amy's mother persisted. "Exactly how do I do that?" she asked.

The response was swift. One mother said, "My daughter takes her cue from me. Whenever I lose my cool and yell at her brother, I hear the same nasty words coming out of her mouth just a little later. But if I say something like, 'Hey Benjy, no biting Mommy! You can bite your blankie or your teddy,' then five minutes later I'll hear her giving him a choice."

A father said, "I try to let my five-year-old know what I expect of him. I've told him, 'I know it isn't easy to be around your sister when she hits, but you can't hit her back. She's still very young and has a lot to learn. But if we all do our job—you, me and Mommy—and teach her better ways to get what she wants, little by little she'll understand what's okay for her to do and what isn't.'"

"Those are all ways to prevent hitting," Amy's mother said, "but I still don't know what to do *after* the older one has hurt her little brother. If punishment isn't the answer, what is?"

"I have a thought," a woman said. "Do you think it would help if you sat down and problem-solved with Amy? Not at the moment of course. And not when you're angry. But after you've comforted the little one. When you're both feeling calmer."

Amy's mother looked skeptical. "Problem solve? . . . With a four-year-old?"

Someone suggested trying an experiment. Would the woman

who proposed problem-solving be willing to pretend to be Amy's mother and show how the conversation might go? And would Amy's mother be willing to play the part of her daughter? Both women agreed. Here's how the scene unfolded as they enacted each step of the problem solving process:

Step 1: Hear the child's point of view.

Mother: Billy made you so mad this morning that you pushed him.

Amy: He's a pest.

Mother: He really annoys you.

Amy: I was making tracks for my train and he kept grabbing them.

Mother: That could be pretty frustrating—someone grabbing your tracks when you're trying to put them together. Is there anything else he does that bothers you?

Amy: He's always taking my toys and he eats my Play-Doh, and he broke my Jack-in-the-Box.

Mother: So he does a lot of things that upset you.

Amy: Yeah!

Step 2: Express your point of view.

Mother: I get very upset when one of my children hurts another.

Step 3: Invite your child to brainstorm with you.

> *Mother:* Let's put our heads together and see whether there's anything we can think of doing when Billy bothers you that will be good for you and good for Billy.

Step 4: Write down all ideas—without evaluating.

> *Amy:* Lock him in his room.
>
> *Mother:* Okay. I'll write that down. What else?
>
> *Amy:* (Laughing now) Tie him to a chair.
>
> *Mother:* I've got that. What else?

The group watched intently as the conversation became serious. "Mother" pointed out that sometimes people in a family make each other mad, but that they need to find ways to live together without hurting each other. Here's the list of solutions that were finally agreed to:

Solutions

1. Push Billy's hand away gently. Say, "I'm playing with this now. I'll tell you when I'm finished so you can have a turn."

2. Give Billy a few pieces of what you're playing with—like a few tracks and a train, or a few blocks.

3. Give Billy a choice of other things he can play with. Say, "You can play with my pegboard or my pounding bench."

4. Play with your things on a high table where Billy can't reach them.

5. Play with some things (like paints or Play-Doh) when Billy takes his nap.

6. If nothing else works, ask for help. Call out, "Mom, I need help!" and Mom will appear.

When the problem solving demonstration came to an end, there were many reactions:

"I don't see why this approach wouldn't work with the real Amy."

"What I like is the way it freed the mother to be on her daughter's side instead of against her."

"I noticed that it wasn't easy for them to come up with things you can realistically do to deal with a toddler. It was hard work to come up with solutions."

"Yes, but it's that work that makes the solutions stick."

Amy's mother listened and beamed at us all. "Know how it was for me?" she asked. By playing Amy, by putting myself in her shoes, I felt for her. And I began to see things from her point of view. I can't wait to get home today so I can play the part of the real mother."

The Stories

The most rewarding part of running workshops for parents of young children were the stories that came back week after week. Here's a sampling of the ones that left us all smiling.

This first story clearly contrasts what happens when typical methods are used to stop a child's misbehavior—orders, threats, warnings—with what can happen the moment feelings are acknowledged. It really is easier for a child to change his behavior when someone accepts his strong feelings.

"I Want Jack's Stick!"

Scene: I am trying to get some gardening done while my three children—four-year-old twins James and Samantha, and two-year-old Jack—play nearby in the yard. I'm crouched far back in a flowerbed next to the house, pulling dead wood off the rhododendron and tossing it over the other bushes onto the lawn. The kids are picking sticks out of the growing pile and playing with them. Suddenly there is conflict.

James: Give me that stick! (Tries to grab stick from little brother.)

Jack: No. My stick. (Runs away from James.)

James: I want it. Let me have it. (Chases Jack and grabs stick.)

Jack: Waaaah! (Manages to hang onto stick.)

Mom: (Pokes head out from behind bushes.) What is going on here?

Jack: James trying take my stick.

Mom: James, leave Jack alone.

James: But I need that stick.

Mom: You don't need Jack's stick. You have your own stick.

James: (Throws his stick down.) This stick is no good.

Mom: Well then, pick a different stick.

James: I don't want a different stick. I want Jack's stick.

Mom: You can't have Jack's stick. He picked it first.

Samantha: Here, James, you want my stick?

James: No, not your stick, Jack's stick. Jack, you gimme that stick right now!

Mom: (Comes out from behind the bushes and paws through the pile of sticks on the lawn.) Look, James, here's a good stick; it has leaves on it. And here's another good one; it's really long.

James: (Shouting) Those are stupid sticks! I don't want those stupid sticks!

Mom: James, if you don't stop screaming this instant, you are going inside the house for a time out.

James: (Still shouting.) I don't need a time out. I need Jack's stick! Jack better give me that stick right now.

Mom: (At last remembers about acknowledging kids' feelings.) James, you really want Jack's stick.

James: Yeah! I want it.

Mom: (Sympathetically) You think Jack's stick is best, and you're disappointed that you can't have it.

James: Yeah . . . yeah. Hey, Samantha, look, a butterfly! Let's chase it. (Runs off after butterfly.)

Mom: (Stands there with mouth open.) Oh, my gosh, it worked!

One mother described her new way of copying when everyone in the family becomes furious with everyone else.

I Use Drama

When the whole family gets angry, I use drama . . . and it works. Last time it happened, I said very loud, "Man, *everybody* is mad! I am mad, Zoe is mad, Till is mad, and Papi is mad. Even the cats are mad! Let's all take a few minutes and then meet for a sweet snack in the dining room." In a few minutes everybody came out of their holes and we sat around a table. I said, "Wow, we just had a complete family explosion happening. It's like four volcanoes erupting, and guess what? We made it! Nobody lost an ear, nobody got kicked with a stinky foot, nobody got taken by Voldemort (*Harry Potter*), and we are all still alive. Wow, we rock!" Everybody started making up things that did not happen to us . . . . and we all laughed.

One parent in the group wrote a note for her child who couldn't read and that started a trend. These next three stories show the power of the written word for the preschool set.

Brothers Are Not for Shoving

My one-year-old is just starting to learn to walk. My three-year-old keeps pushing him down. One day I decided to scotch tape a sign onto the back of the baby's T-shirt. It said, "Brothers are for loving—not for shoving." Then I read the sign to the three-year-old, and he actually stopped knocking his brother over.

Letter from a Baby Sister

My five-year-old daughter had a cold and so I asked her to stay away from the new baby. As the day wore on I told her over and over again to keep away from the baby, but to no avail. Finally, I decided to write a note to her as if it were written by the baby. Here's what I wrote:

Dear Elizabeth,

When you are better, you can hold me as much as you want.

Love,
Emily

Elizabeth was thrilled with the note. She had me read it to her at least fifteen to twenty times over the next few days. And she stayed away from the baby.

"I Want a Sign, Too!"

I was going crazy. Every morning between four and six A.M., my two-and-a-half-year-old son, Spencer, would climb out of his bed and climb into the baby's crib and wake him up because he wanted to "play" with him. The baby, nine-month-old Russell, would then start to scream. That would be my cue to run into the room, pull Spencer out and give him a smack on his behind. That made Spencer scream and then the baby would scream even louder. This went on for weeks.

One day I read the part in *How to Talk So Kids Will Listen* . . . about writing notes to children who were too young to read and thought, "What have I got to lose?" So, I said to Spencer, "Russell can't write. He needs someone to help make a sign for his crib. You're older and you can write. I gave him crayons and paper, and he scribbled on it. Then I wrote on the same page: *This is Russell's crib. All others keep out.*

Then I taped the sign on the wall over the baby's crib. Spencer asked me, "What does it say?" I read it to him. Then he said, "I want a sign, too." Together we made a sign that read: *This is Spencer's bed. All others keep out.*

Believe it or not, it worked! Every morning now Spencer points to the sign over the baby's crib and says, "Keep out." And now the baby, who's begun to talk, imitates his brother and says, "Kee-ow!"

This last story shows how a mother invited a three-year-old to take responsibility for her behavior.

I Like to Bite

I was at my wit's end. Carrie (3) had recently begun to bite her sister, Alice (5), and nothing I said or did stopped her. It seemed a little crazy to try problem-solving with a three-year-old, but I was desperate. The morning after last week's workshop, I took out a piece of paper and told them both that I was going to write down all their feelings about biting. Carrie, the biter, was thrilled, but Alice, the "bitee," said, "That's stupid!"

Here's what Carrie told me to put down (it was hard for me to keep a straight face while I was writing):

I like to bite.

Biting feels good.

Biting is fun.

Then Alice said, "I want a list, too!" For her I wrote, *Alice gets angry when her sister bites her and doesn't know why she does it.*

Then we made up a *Solutions* list. It included things like:

Bite food.

Use words.

Walk away.

Since then, every time Carrie starts to bite, Alice will yell, "The list! Remember the list!" And Carrie just stops in her tracks and shrinks back. It's amazing—like holding up a cross to a vampire. Once Carrie ran to the refrigerator and came back with an apple between her teeth. Another time in the supermarket when she was especially frustrated, she tried to bite me on my leg, but all in all, she's definitely getting better.

II. Home Alone

The parents in our workshops who had older children had different concerns. Many of the mothers and fathers were out of the house and into the workplace. Most of the single parents in our group had no choice but to leave their school-age kids home alone until they returned from work. There were long hours when no one was around to monitor the children. No responsible adult was in charge to guide, prevent, restrain, stop, or redirect one sibling's hurtful or violent behavior toward another. Even when parents were at work, they were worried about what was going on at home. For the stepparents in our workshops, the problems were compounded. Each set of siblings left alone had to mesh their different family rules, dynamics, values, lifestyles, and personalities, and somehow function together as one reasonably cooperative unit.

The general consensus in our groups was that in the brief time the parents did have with their children, they needed to seize every opportunity to nurture relationships and teach their children and stepchildren how to deal with one another civilly and safely.

As our meetings continued, parents told many stories of how they were able to put their new skills and convictions into action. Here are some of the most memorable experiences they shared.

You Need to Tell Him Yourself

The only way I can explain why I'm so excited about what happened yesterday is to start by telling you what I usually do when Jill (she's eleven) complains to me about David (he's thirteen). Here's how a typical conversation would go:

Jill: (First thing out of her mouth as I get home from work): Ma, David is so mean. I hate him!

Me: Why? Calm down. What happened? What did he do?

Jill: He kicked me out of his room. Just because his dumb friends were over. He said, "Get out of here, pest."

Me: Well, were you pestering him?

Jill: No! All I did was ask him to lend me his eraser and he wouldn't give it to me.

Me: What?! He wouldn't lend you an eraser?

Jill: No. And I needed it for my homework.

Me: Well, I'm going to have a few words with your

brother tonight. Don't you worry, sweetheart. He's never going to do that again.

Jill: Good! You tell him.

But I didn't say any of that. I did a complete turn-around. I didn't take sides; I didn't try to judge who's right, or who's wrong; and I didn't yell at David. Instead, I tried doing a lot of the things I learned here, and that changed everything. So here's what really happened:

Jill: David is so mean. I hate him!

Me: Uh-oh, he must have done something that made you really angry.

Jill: He kicked me out of his room. He said, "Get out of here, pest."

Me: That must have hurt your feelings.

Jill: It did! And he said it in front of all his friends.

Me: That could be embarrassing.

Jill: It was! He could have told me nicely.

Me: (I had to think a long time before I came up with this and I said it very slowly.) So, you want David to know that if he wants to be alone with his friends, he can say it in a nice way—without calling you names.

Jill: Yeah . . . or without shoving me. So you tell him that.

Me: (Now this is the part I'm most proud of.) Honey, if it comes from me, it will just make him madder at you. You need to tell him yourself—what you told me just now. You said it very clearly. He doesn't have to embarrass you or push you. If he wants to be alone with his friends, all he has to do is ask you to leave in a nice way and you'll go.

   "Well, she didn't look too happy about that, but she didn't argue with me. And even if she had, it wouldn't have thrown me. I know I'm on the right track. By giving her the actual words to use to tell her brother what bothers her, I'm showing her how to approach him in a way that won't cause a worse argument between them when I'm not around."

Put It in Writing

I thought that by the time my son and daughter were in their teens I wouldn't have to be dealing with "sibling stuff" anymore. But recently they've been so vile to each other, it's impossible to be in the same house with them. And it's gotten worse since my wife went back to work. The minute I walk through the door, before I even put down my briefcase, each tries to get me aside to complain about the other.

   Last night though, I was ready for them. I listened quietly for a while. Then I handed each of them a pencil and paper and said, "Listen, you two. I can hear that there are a lot of things about each other that really bother you. I'd like you to put them in writing. And be sure to number them according to importance."

They went for it. They both sat down at the kitchen table and started writing furiously. I left the room. When I came back about ten minutes later, I saw my daughter had listed seven complaints about her brother. He had four items on his paper and they were both still writing. I went into the den to finish a report on my computer.

The next morning, as I was getting ready to leave for work, I heard a strange sound in the house—laughter. And numbers being shouted out.

"Two!"

"Yeah, but seven."

"No, five!"

"And don't forget three!"

More laughter.

I finally figured out that the numbers were shorthand for what they had written. It's not the way most people communicate, but for these two it was the first break in the cold war.

Repeat and Erase

The best thing for me about these workshops was the idea that you don't have to take sides when kids fight. But I had some strong doubts about what you recommended— to just stand there and repeat the main idea of what each one is trying to say. Well, last week I had a chance to find out. Here's what actually happened:

I was in the middle of getting dressed to go to work when I heard screaming from the girls' bedroom. I rushed in and saw them shoving each other.

Me: Hold it! Boy, you two are mad at each other!

Carol (12): She won't let me get my socks!

Me: Amy, Carol says you won't let her get her socks.

Amy (10): Oh yeah, sure! I was taking out my tights and she closed the drawer on me. She could've broken my hand.

Me: Carol, Amy says you closed the drawer on her.

Carol: How else was I supposed to get my socks? Besides, I had my drawer opened first.

Me: Amy, Carol says her drawer was opened first.

Amy: Sure it was opened, but she wasn't there. What was I supposed to do? Stand around until Her Royal Highness decided to come back?

This was hard work—reflecting what each one said to the other. It was also a big mess. I wasn't even sure I understood what they were talking about. Then I remembered the "erase" story in *Liberated Parents/Liberated Children.*

Me: Do you know what I do when I get into a tangle like this with someone and it just seems hopeless that we'll ever be able to straighten it out? I erase the whole thing and start all over again. (I make an erasing motion on the wall.) Okay, the slate is clean. You can start from the beginning. I'm leaving. Lots of luck.

I left the room and closed the door, but I must confess that I hung around outside to eavesdrop. Here's what I heard:

Carol: Okay, Amy, now you say, "Carol, dear, did you want to get your socks from this open drawer?" And I'll say, "That's okay, sister dear. You take your tights first."

Amy: Sister dear! That's dumb. Hand me my tights. I'm late for school.

That was it. It was over.

My hope is they'll remember the idea of "erasing" and use it when I'm not around.

The Mood Box

I realized that one of the reasons my son and stepson didn't get along, even though they're both ten, was their insensitivity to each other's moods. When one was grumpy, the other was cheerful. When one wanted to be alone, the other wanted to play. I could always see the big blowup coming, but neither one of them seemed to have a clue about what the other was feeling. When I was home I could help them understand each other's moods, but what about the times I wasn't available to play interpreter?

Then I remembered reading in *Liberated Parents/Liberated Children* about the child who had made a mood box. I decided to make each of the boys a six-sided mood box out of construction paper and tape, with each of the six sides a different color. The colors were meant to represent different moods. When the boys saw what I was doing, they became interested and helped me make up a color key. Here's what they decided on:

Grey	=	Tired
Blue	=	Disappointed
Red	=	Angry
Black	=	Rotten
Yellow	=	Happy
Green	=	Okay

The plan was to let the rest of the family know "where you were at" by turning your color face out.

So far the kids have been using it. One day Ben came home and seemed shocked. He said, "Brian's box is on black! What happened?" I explained that Brian had had a bad day at Little League, and I noticed that afterward Ben tried to be extra nice to him.

Another time Brian came into the kitchen and said, "Uh-oh, I'd better not ask Ben for his baseball glove now. His box is on red."

Those two small boxes have made a big difference in our sons' lives. In fact, it's helped all of us—my husband included—to become more sensitive to each other.

III. More Ways to Encourage
Good Feelings Between
Brothers and Sisters

Out of the many workshops we ran following the publication of *Siblings Without Rivalry,* there came a number of new ideas and greater clarity about some old ideas. Here's what we felt was especially important for all parents to know:

Make sure that each child gets some time alone with you several times a week.

In today's rushed, impersonal world, some time alone is essential. Children thrive on the warmth and intimacy of private moments with their parents. This one-on-one connection provides the emotional nourishment kids need to be more caring or at the very least more tolerant of their siblings. Johnny is less likely to pick a fight with his sister to get you to notice him if he knows there will be time set aside when he will have "just you" listening to "just him."

Once you set the time aside for "just the two of you," honor it. Don't let a phone call break the mood. Your child will always remember your saying, "Hello, Mrs. Jones. May I call you back in fifteen minutes? Right now, Johnny and I are spending time together." Chances are, after Johnny has had you so completely to himself, he will be more generously disposed toward his siblings. But even more important, he will have a greater sense of his own value. One mother told us:

I came home from the group last week determined to do something about Kevin, my middle boy. He's the one who sort of slips between the cracks, a typical middle child, neither here nor there. Well, the next morning I asked him if he'd keep me company while I was doing some errands, and he seemed happy to come along. We were talking in the car, and I thought everything was just great, when suddenly he dropped a bombshell. He said, "I wish I weren't me. I wish I were Robert or David."

I didn't know what to say, so I asked him, "How come?"

He said, "Robert gets to do whatever he wants and everybody 'goo-goos' over David."

I started to tell him that he shouldn't feel that way, but I stopped myself. I said, "Well, maybe you'd like to be David or Robert, but I wouldn't like it at all."

He said, "Why not?"

I said, "Because you're very special. And if you became anyone else in the family, then I wouldn't have *you* anymore . . . I wouldn't have my Kevin. And that would make me miserable!"

You know what he did? He reached over and patted my shoulder.

Afterwards, I told myself that one afternoon with him wasn't going to do it. Kevin needed a lot more time with me. And a lot more time with his father. He needed both of us to beam back at him a feeling of *his* importance.

When spending time with one child, don't talk about the other.

On your shopping trip with Mary, keep the focus on Mary. Refrain from: "Look at this blue sweater. It'll look great on your sister, with her blue eyes!" or "Oh, Debbie would love this Snoopy button! Let's buy it for her collection."

The parent means no harm. She might even feel she's encouraging the children to be thoughtful of each other. But more likely Mary will think, "Even when Debbie isn't here, she takes Mom away from me."

Don't withhold your affection or attention from your "favorite child" in order to make it up to a less favored child.

Some parents experience such guilt when they admit to themselves that they feel partial toward one child, that they go to the other extreme. In a misguided effort to even things out, they shower exaggerated praise and attention upon their less favored child and become distant or cool toward the child who speaks to their heart. This sudden shift can only cause confusion and hurt to both children. One thinks, "What's wrong? What have I done? My parent doesn't love me anymore." And the other child senses that "something isn't right . . . something doesn't feel real."

All each child needs from a parent is a full and realistic appreciation for who he or she is.

Don't lock the children into their position in the family constellation (oldest, youngest, middle). Allow each child the opportunity to experience some of the privileges and responsibilities of the other.

Part of what creates deep resentment between siblings is the demand by parents that they always maintain their family position. We can't reverse the children's order in the family. But neither do we have to keep them playing out their birth order roles forever. Here, in their own words, is what some of the parents in our workshops have done:

My girls (nine and five) are classic examples of super-serious oldest and babyish youngest types. This Saturday I did something I've never done before. I called my sister and asked her to switch with me. I told her I'd take her two-year-old if she would take my nine-year-old for the afternoon and let her play with her teenage cousins.

Well, both my girls had a wonderful experience. My five-year-old was busy all afternoon playing "big sister" to her two-year-old cousin, acting very important and grown-up; and my nine-year-old came home bubbling with excitement about how nice her cousins had been to her. They had decked her out in some old junk jewelry, fluffed out her hair, and showed her how to do the Macarena. She loved being fussed over and made the center of attention.

• • •

SINCE THE BIRTH of my second child, my oldest daughter has been asking to play "baby" and I don't discourage her anymore. I used to feel peculiar about a four-year-old wanting a bottle all the time. But recently I've been playing along with her. I bought her this toy bottle and filled it with water and I said, "Do you want your bottle now, baby? Okay, here it is." Once I asked her, "Do you want to be the baby or should I?" Then we took turns giving each other the bottle. She got such a kick out of it, she wanted to do it everyday for a week. Then one day while we were playing the "baby game," she put down the bottle and said, "Now let's play dress-up."

• • •

ONE EVENING before supper, I told my ten-year-old daughter not to bother to set the table but to just relax and enjoy her book. Then I asked my six-year-old son to help me put away the groceries and set the table. He was thrilled. He felt like such a big shot. And my oldest daughter was very happy not to have to be the one who always helps me around the house.

Don't get trapped by "togetherness."

The picture of a whole family enjoying an outing together is appealing. But for some children the pressure of having to spend long stretches of time in the company of a brother or sister can put additional stress upon an already strained relationship. (Not to mention what extended time with bickering children can do to the nerves of parents.)

Take a beautiful day at the zoo: The little ones rushes to keep up with the big one. The big one runs ahead and calls the little one a "slowpoke." (Tears.) The little one wants to stop to eat. The big one isn't hungry yet. Both complain, "Why do we always have to do what *he* wants to do?" (Fight.) The big one wants to see the snakes. The little one is afraid of snakes. (Fight and tears.) The little one is suddenly tired and wants to go home. The big one is mad. He still hasn't seen the snakes. (More fighting. More tears.)

We suggest that if children are going through a period where there's constant irritation between them, the parents ought not subject them to "togetherness." It could only serve to drive them further apart.

Instead, it might be better to consider planning different kinds of adult-child combinations:

Dad can take one child out while Mom stays home with the other.

Mom can take a child out while Dad stays home with the other.

Everybody goes to the zoo, splits up, and meets for lunch.

Anything to give everyone more breathing space.

Let each child know what it is about him that his siblings like or admire.

Very often two children will behave like sworn enemies because they're unaware of the underlying feelings of admiration and affection that one has for the other. Just knowing about a sibling's positive feelings can make for a dramatic shift in a relationship. A father in our group shared the following childhood experience:

My sisters and I had a battle going on all the time. It was brutal for all of us, probably especially for my parents. How did they diffuse it? How did they get me to stop belting my little sisters? They said, "Scott, listen: You do realize that your younger sisters think the world of you. They just admire you so much and they try to impress you with the things they do." Now that just set me back. So the next time I was ready to belt them I thought, "Well, maybe my parents are right." And that seemed to calm me down. It stopped me anyway.

• • •

NOT TILL I was grown up and had an all-night heart-to-heart talk with my brother did I realize how much pain could have been prevented—on both our parts—if we had really known how we felt about each other when we were kids. Because he was my older brother, he was like a God to me—handsome, popular, a talented musician. I could never understand why he was always so cruel and mean to me. I was sure it was because he hated me. And so, even though I admired him so much, I mustered every ounce of my strength to fight him. I felt I had to do everything in my power to get back at him—to hurt him before he could hurt me.

But to hear him tell it, it was a completely different story. He said he always thought that I was terrific—pretty and super smart, and he felt so awed by my grades and so inadequate as a student and so ashamed of himself for his own poor grades, that he got back at me in the only way he knew how—by teasing and being mean. And I got back at him by cutting him to ribbons with my intellect and sarcasm. If somehow either one of us had been made aware of the great affection and admiration that we each felt for the other, it would have been a big help to both of us.

When I told this to my mother, she became defensive.

She said, "Why would I have to tell either one of you how the other felt? It was obvious to me that underneath it all you really loved each other."

But it sure wasn't obvious to us.

Schedule family meetings.

You wouldn't expect your car to run without periodic refueling and maintenance, yet we expect our family unit to run without regular checkups. The most enthusiastic endorsement for family meetings comes from parents and children who have experienced them. One teenager told us, "It's a great way to make sure tensions never build up. We sit around and talk about family activities, chores, who wants to do what, who wants to trade off what, who's bothered by what." His mother added, "It's a time for all of us to think creatively about what we need for ourselves and how we can be supportive of each other."

In one family, Dad brought up how unnerved he had been during recent car rides by the screaming and squabbling in the backseat and asked for ideas to make sure the ride would be safe and pleasant for everyone. The suggestions flew: bring books, play games, tell jokes, ask riddles, sing songs. But best of all was the growing resolve in the family to make care rides less stressful for Dad.

In another family, with six children and little money, the kids decided to do each other's chores on their birthdays as their gift to each other.

One mother recently wrote to tell us about her very first family meeting. She reported:

I wanted to make it fun so I wrote a separate invitation to my six-year-old and seven-year-old:

A FAMILY MEETING
Place: Dining Room Table
Time: Friday 6:30 P.M.
Dress: Casual
We need *you!*

The response from the girls was not encouraging. They said, "Oh, I'm not going." "What are we going to talk about?" "What's a meeting?" "How do you dress casual?" "I'm going to bring that up at our family meeting."

The day came. Dad insisted that the meeting be in the living room where it was more comfortable. My opening topic was the escape route in case of fire. We discussed all the precautions we needed to take. After that we talked about various family concerns: Who would walk the dog on school mornings and what movie to rent this weekend. Then there was a moment of silence. Our seven-year-old said, "You know, I think this is a great family. I'm really happy I'm in it." Our six-year-old chimed in, "Me too. I like our family." It brought tears to my eyes. Something so simple as a family meeting had such an effect! And it only took fifteen minutes. That night we all felt a special closeness.

Conclusion

We hope this new chapter will be helpful to you. Although it shows how sibling relationships can be improved, sometimes dramatically, by skillful adult intervention, it helps to remember that not all our interventions work out perfectly or permanently.

Sibling relationships are fluid, changing, constantly in process. At different periods of their lives, brothers and sisters draw apart or come together. There is no way that we as parents can mandate a fixed, close, loving relationship between our children. However, what we can do, with skills and goodwill, is remove the usual obstacles to sibling harmony, so that when our children are ready to reach out to one another, the road is clear.

The challenge is difficult. But it is merely difficult. It is not impossible. We need to deal with our own feelings, help our children to deal with their feelings, and somehow take all the raw, angry, confusing emotions generated by sibling rivalry and use them. Yes, use them to grow into more sensitive, aware, caring human beings. Use them to learn how to live together despite deep differences.

The family is where we learn our relationship skills. And the way we relate to our children and teach them to relate to each other, even in the heat of battle, can be our permanent gift to them.

Brothers and Sisters, After All

by Adele Faber and Elaine Mazlish,
from *Between Brothers and Sisters*

Mother . . . Father . . . Child
A tight little universe
of nurturers and nurtured
of dreamers and the dream come true.
A circle of love.

Why break it?
Why another child?
(or two or three or more)
Only for the moment, to make the circle wider.
More warmth. More joy.

Brothers and sisters laughing and loving
Shaping their childhood from a hundred happy
    happenings
Confidants and friends
A Bulwark. Strong and safe together
in a cold, indifferent world.
There for each other when we no longer are.
Sweet vision of sibling harmony!

You'll see, you'll love the baby.
It will be your baby, too.

No!

It's here!
Born.
Who is this stranger?
What is a "brother"?
What is a "sister"?
A ROBBER
of time for only two
A THIEF
of arms and laps
A STEALER
of songs and stories and smiles for you alone.

Go away, stranger.
Get lost and never be found.
Not ever!

But if it has to stay, then what's the way?

BE IT!

Wet your bed
suck your thumb
and cry, cry, cry.
Or
Hit it. Kiss it. Bite it. Tease it. Play with it.

Play with it?
Peek-a-boo
Mush in the mud
Push on the swing
Pull in the wagon
It's my turn, crybaby.

Mother is having another?
Not again!

WHY?
Even less for us now.

Oh well . . . let's play.
Wrestle and tumble
Hide-and-Go-Seek
Race down the hill
I won!

Marbles
Checkers
Pick-Up Sticks
Crazy-Eights . . . Gin Rummy . . . War
Cheater! Liar! Get out of my room!

Let's go to the beach
Skate on the pond
Hang out in the street
We're having a party
No, you can't come. My friends don't want you.
When did he grow taller
than me?
When did she get prettier
than me?
He's so smart. Mom likes him best.
She's so sweet. Daddy's little darling.
They're disgusting!

But
you can tell her private things
and she won't tell
And he will help you with your math
And she defends you when Dad yells
And he'll lend his camera if you're "careful."
And she listens when you give advice
And he protects you from the bully on the block.

Scattered now
Busy now
Different schools, different paths.
A letter . . . now and then
A phone call . . . now and then.

Back home for the holidays.
Hugs and Happiness.
You look terrific!
When did you cut your hair?
When did you grow a beard?
The table is beautiful.
Everything smells so good.
Home, home at last.
Each in his accustomed chair.

You still eat like a pig . . .
Only kidding.
You still act like a jerk . . .
Only kidding.

Children, children!

So you dropped math. That figures.
You think you know me, don't you?
He's only showing off.
As usual.

Now children, that's enough!

Two people sitting in each sibling seat
The adult that is
The child that was
Locked into the past.
When will we see each other as we are?
As we are striving to become?

Sorry if I hurt you.
I guess I was thinking how you always used to . . .
But that's because you always used to . . .
I never did.
You did too.
Well, if I did, it was because I felt . . .
I didn't know that.
Well now you do.
Oh.

Grown up at last!
Rivalries behind us. No need to compete.
Homes of our own
Work of our own
Loves of our own.
My brother, the teacher, makes less money.
My sister, the nurse, has more children.
My children are smarter than her children.
My house is bigger than his house.

What do we do about Mom?
Can't put her in a nursing home.
She'd never go.
I'd never let her.
Maybe you could take her
Why me?
You're her favorite.
I had her for a month this summer.
But I'm the one who sees her every day.

Our children are grown.
Our parents are gone.

We remain.
My brother, my sister, myself.

So strange. He turns his graying head and laughs
and there's the boy again.
She gestures with a wrinkled hand
and there's the girl again.
Do you remember when . . .
Oh yes, oh yes! Do <u>you</u> remember when . . . ?

My brother, my sister, myself.
You went to the doctor?
What did he say?
Another opinion?
I'm here if you need me.

Comforters for our todays
Guardians of memories
Keeping our youth and yesterdays alive
Comrades with one history.

No one cares
who is better
who is worse
who has more
who has less.
Content in our connectedness
we are brothers and sisters
after all.

Additional Reading That May Be Helpful

Balter, Lawrence, and Anita Shreve. *Dr. Balter's Child Sense: Understanding and Handling the Common Problems of Infancy and Early Childhood.* New York: Poseidon Press, 1985.

A warm and gentle guide for parents of young children with some practical suggestions for easing children over the "new baby" hurdle.

Bank, Stephen P., and Michael D. Kahn. *The Sibling Bond.* New York: Basic Books, 1982.

A fascinating exploration of the many varieties of sibling relationships and of the tremendous impact that brothers and sisters have upon each other's lives.

Baruch, Dorothy Walter. *New Ways in Discipline.* New York: McGraw-Hill, 1949.

A groundbreaking book with a wealth of creative ideas for helping children cope with their "mean- mad" feelings toward their siblings.

Faber, Adele, and Elaine Mazlish. *Liberated Parents, Liberated Children: Your Guide to a Happier Family* New York: HarperCollins, 2004.

A personal account of the authors' early years in a workshop directed by Dr. Haim Ginott, with many examples of handling sibling trouble spots woven into the story.

Faber, Adele, and Elaine Mazlish. *How to Talk So Kids Will Listen & Listen So Kids Will Talk.* New York: Scribner, 2012.

Recommended for two reasons:

1. Much of the "bossy" or hurtful language that siblings use with each other is a direct result of how mom or dad speak to them. *How to Talk* . . . provides a model of respectful communication that most parents would be pleased to hear their children use when talking to each other.

2. Children who think well of themselves are less likely to attack their siblings and more likely to be helpful to them. All the skills in *How to Talk* . . . build self-esteem.

Ginott, Haim. *Between Parent and Child*. New York: Three Rivers Press, 2003.

Has a clearly written chapter on the origins of jealousy between children—the attitudes that foster it and how to deal with it. Also has a good description of children who need psychotherapy because of intense sibling rivalry.

Kohn, Alfie. *No Contest: The Case Against Competition*. New York: Houghton Mifflin, 1986.

A provocative, carefully researched challenge to our culture's widely held beliefs about the value of competition.

Meyer, Donald J., and Patricia F. Vadasy. *Sibshops: Workshops for Siblings of Children with Special Needs*. Baltimore, Md: Paul H. Brooks Publishing Company, 2000.

Innovative ways to comfort and empower children whose siblings have special needs.

Orlick, Terry. *Winning Through Cooperation—Competitive Insanity: Cooperative Alternatives*. Washington, D.C.: Hawkins and Assoc., 1977.

Competitive games can be a major source of sibling stress. A whole new world of good feelings and team spirit opens up when children and family join in cooperative games.

Reit, Seymour V. *Sibling Rivalry.* The Bank Street College of Education Child Development Series. New York: Ballantine, 1985.

A look at the problems created by sibling rivalry along with some sound ideas on how to cope. A good description of the special problems faced by twins and stepchildren.

Stark, Vikki. *My Sister, Myself.* New York: McGraw-Iill, 2007.

A fascinating study of how profoundly sisters shape each other's lives.

For Further Study

If you are interested in a chance to practice and further explore the skills and ideas in this book with others, you can send for information about the six-session "Siblings Without Rivalry Workshop Kit" created by Adele Faber and Elaine Mazlish. The kit consists of a chairperson's guide, parents' workbooks, materials for role-plays, and CDs of the authors conducting each workshop session. For additional details, please visit our Web site, www.fabermazlish .com, or contact us directly:

info@fabermazlish.com

1-800-944-8454

Faber/Mazlish Workshops, LLC
P.O. Box 1072
Carmel, NY 10512

Index

Page numbers in *italics* refer to cartoons.

About Adele Faber and Elaine Mazlish

Internationally acclaimed experts on communication between adults and children, Adele Faber and Elaine Mazlish have produced a body of work that has won the gratitude of parents and the enthusiastic praise of the professional community.

Their first book, *Liberated Parents/Liberated Children*, received the Christopher Award for "literary achievement affirming the highest values of the human spirit." Their subsequent books, *How To Talk So Kids Will Listen & Listen So Kids Will Talk* and *Siblings Without Rivalry* (#1 on the *New York Times* bestseller list), have sold over four million copies and have been translated into more than thirty languages. *How To Talk So Kids Can Learn—at Home and at School* was cited by *Child* magazine as the "best book of the year for excellence in family issues in education." Their most recent book, *How to Talk So Teens Will Listen & Listen So Teens Will Talk*, tackles the tough problems of the teenage years. The authors' group workshop programs are currently being used by parent and teacher groups around the world to improve relationships with children.

Both authors studied with the late child psychologist Dr. Haim Ginott and are former members of the faculty of the New School for Social Research in New York and the Family Life Institute of Long Island University. In addition to their lectures throughout the United States, Canada, and abroad, they have appeared on every major television talk show from *Oprah* to *Good Morning America*. They currently reside on Long Island, New York, and each is the parent of three children.